The short guide to social policy

John Hudson, Stefan Kühner and Stuart Lowe

First published in Great Britain in 2008 by

The Policy Press
University of Bristol
Fourth Floor
Beacon House
Queen's Road
Bristol BS8 1QU
UK

Tel +44 (0)117 331 4054
Fax +44 (0)117 331 4093
e-mail tpp-info@bristol.ac.uk
www.policypress.org.uk

British Library Cataloguing in Publication Data
A catalogue record for this book is available from the British Library.

Library of Congress Cataloging-in-Publication Data
A catalog record for this book has been requested.

ISBN 978 1 84742 061 9 paperback

Cover design by In-Text Design, Bristol.
Printed and bound in Great Britain by Henry Ling Ltd, Dorchester.

Contents

List of tables, figures and boxes

Boxes

General abbreviations

€	Euro
ALMP	Active labour market policy
AUS$	Australian dollars
DKK	Danish Kroner
EU	European Union
Eurostat	The Statistical Office of the European Communities
GDP	Gross Domestic Product: a measure of economic output that represents the total size of a nation's economy
ILO	International Labour Organization
IMF	International Monetary Fund
NZ$	New Zealand dollars
OECD	Organisation for Economic Co-operation and Development
PISA	Programme for International Student Assessment
Quango	Quasi-autonomous non-governmental organisation
SEK	Swedish Krona
TANF	Temporary Assistance for Needy Families
UN	United Nations
UNDP	United Nations Development Programme
UNESCO	United Nations Educational, Scientific and Cultural Organization
US$	US dollars

Country abbreviations

AUS	Australia	KOR	Korea (South)
AUT	Austria	LTU	Lithuania
BEL	Belgium	LUX	Luxembourg
CAN	Canada	LVA	Latvia
CHL	Chile	MEX	Mexico
COL	Colombia	NET	Netherlands
CYP	Cyprus	NOR	Norway
CZE	Czech Republic	NZ	New Zealand
DEN	Denmark	PHL	Philippines
EST	Estonia	POL	Poland
FIN	Finland	POR	Portugal
FRA	France	ROM	Romania
GER	Germany	SGP	Singapore
GRE	Greece	SPA	Spain
HKG	Hong Kong, China (SAR)	SVK	Slovakia
HUN	Hungary	SVN	Slovenia
IRE	Ireland	SWE	Sweden
ISL	Iceland	SWI	Switzerland
ISR	Israel	TUR	Turkey
ITA	Italy	UK	United Kingdom
JAP	Japan	US	United States

Preface

This textbook arose from the demand of our students at the University of York for a concise, straightforward and clear account of the subject matter of social policy and, in particular, the requests of our overseas students who often came to us with questions not only about social policy but also about why so many of their introductory textbooks excluded consideration of any case but the UK (and, indeed, why much of the teaching they received did too!).

We were quickly able to show all of our students that social policy is an interdisciplinary subject that draws on the knowledge base and concepts of the core social sciences with a focus on the analysis of social problems. After this the perennial burning question remains: 'what is social policy?'. The answer to this is that there are many different definitions and explanations of the subject but when forced by our students to make a decision about where they might best begin, we have increasingly felt that going 'back to basics' offers a good starting point. This short guide to social policy focuses on the 'pillars of the welfare state' and echoes the subject in its earliest days of development in the UK, following the setting up of the National Health Service, the state education system, a universal social security system, a massive programme of state housing and a commitment to full employment, all the product of the aftermath of the Second World War when people expected benefits from the trauma, losses and struggle of war. People were promised a new society and out of the ashes rose the 'welfare state'. While being aware that this apparently simple and even naïve solution is itself full of pitfalls and would be unlikely to satisfy many of our colleagues who might well approach the subject very differently, seen from the perspective of students brand new to the subject, the demand for a short overview of some key building blocks is perfectly understandable.

However, while we take our inspiration from the UK case, we have tried to broaden the scope of our reflections by drawing on examples and evidence from more than 70 countries. While our writing still betrays our Western European mindset, we have tried hard to offer a less ethnocentric treatment of social policy, not least because we believe there is much to be gained from reflecting on how social policies differ across nations. Indeed, we have discovered from our students that in many ways the UK 'welfare state' is quite odd and the assumption in much of the literature that the 'Beveridge model of welfare' is a kind of default against which other countries might be judged and compared is mistaken. Looking comparatively helps us to see our own countries more clearly and to recognise that one key dimension of social policy ought to be a comparative analysis.

As an introductory text, this book is mostly descriptive, but it does have an implicit, inner, theoretical structure that is central to its approach: each chapter has a common set of headings and themes and so analyses the core pillars of welfare in a more systematic manner than is often the case in introductions to the subject. While the pillars of welfare are quite different from each other in what they do, we feel it is still possible to analyse them through a common conceptual lens. Indeed, we believe that theory is key to further understanding and in the final chapter the whole tone changes to become much more intentionally conceptual, where social policy theory is upfront, acting as a springboard for readers to move up a gear and broaden their own thinking about this fascinating and immediately urgent subject matter.

We would like to take the opportunity to thank staff at The Policy Press, particularly Philip de Bary, Leila Ebrahimi, Jo Morton, Alison Shaw and Emily Watt, for all their encouragement, advice and hard work during the development of this text. Several anonymous referees also gave up valuable time to offer advice about the book, but what is written between these covers is entirely our own. We would also like to thank Dominic Richardson of the OECD for his assistance and ideas. Finally we would like to offer thanks to the many students, who it has been our great pleasure to teach and who often become our friends, for their support. Even though they may not know it their encouragement to commit our ideas to paper is the main reason for this text.

John Hudson, Stefan Kühner and Stuart Lowe
York, December 2007

1

introduction

The ubiquity of social policy

Turn on the television news, pick up a newspaper, visit a news agency website or scan the blogosphere and you will inevitably hear about social policy issues almost instantly.

On 5 October 2007, we sat down to write this introduction and spent an hour or two browsing websites and newspapers from around the world. It was a randomly chosen day, yet the sheer number of social policy-related stories we came across clearly illustrated the fundamental importance of social policy. Furthermore, the controversies embedded in those stories demonstrated in a very human way the reason why social policy engages people in intense debate so readily, even if they often do not realise that 'social policy' is the subject of so many of their everyday conversations. Such was the number of stories we found that we can only give you a small flavour of them here.

One of the starkest stories came from the United States (US), where policy makers were bitterly divided over proposals to increase the number of children covered by health insurance. Just days after 12-year-old Deamonte Driver had died because his family could not afford treatment for a tooth infection, politicians from both main political parties voted to extend coverage to families. President Bush, however, vetoed the reforms on the grounds that they created undue state interference in the healthcare market. The President's opponents did not have to look far for arguments to support reform, for it was announced on that same day that the largest ever study of the health of children in the US was to be extended because of deep concerns about the children's health. Meanwhile, in Costa Rica, it was reported that 'health tourism' is on the rise in its capital San José, with growing numbers of US citizens travelling south for treatment in their Latin American neighbour because they are unable to afford the costs of healthcare in North America.

Healthcare was also a matter of debate in many other countries that day. In the United Kingdom (UK), the government was under pressure to review access to experimental new treatments after it was revealed that a terminally ill charity-fundraising hero had been denied access to a new cancer-fighting drug in the final weeks of her life. In Malaysia, the Deputy Prime Minister called on the country's richer members to donate more money to healthcare charities' causes in order to help extend access of services to the country's poorest people. In Australia, there were concerns that declining support from the federal government meant that individuals were having to contribute more to the costs of healthcare from their own income, putting some services out of reach of some people. Meanwhile, politicians in New Zealand were debating whether the fees paid by patients for visits to family doctors should be determined by the free market rather than being fixed at an agreed rate by the state, even if this meant that some people could be priced out of some services.

There were many concerns about pensions and retirement. In Hungary, there was continued debate about pension reform: while the government agreed that more money needed to be put aside to meet its current pension commitments, an increase in retirement ages seemed a strong possibility in the future in order to help keep costs down. On a similar note, in Singapore, there were reports that Singaporeans were increasingly worried about the future as awareness over the costs of retirement increases. Likewise, in Greece, the head of a government-appointed committee warned that the country faces one of the biggest deficit problems in the world due to its expansive pension system and that reform is needed soon. In Reykjavík, Iceland, meanwhile, the city government approved plans to hire workers aged 70 years old and over in an attempt to address the shortage of workers in some key public services.

Employment and employment issues featured prominently in the news in many countries. In South Africa, the biggest story of the week was the two-day long mission to rescue more than 3,200 gold miners trapped underground in a mineshaft. While all were eventually rescued, the event produced a vigorous debate on workplace safety, with the country's Minerals and Energy Minister seeking sharp improvements in safety through consultation with mining companies, unions and government. In Germany, a study observing family-friendliness in German cities uncovered vast differences across the country, with some cities offering a much better work–life balance than others. Elsewhere in Germany, political parties continued to debate the question of how best to support the country's unemployed. Reforms in 2005 had reduced the amount of time people could claim unemployment insurance, with the goal of getting people back into work more quickly, but the negative social consequences of this decision had led some political figures to argue that the reforms were not working and should be cancelled. In Azerbaijan, meanwhile, a parliamentary commission recommended tough new laws to prevent people from evading social insurance contributions, following fears that many workers were not paying the full amount into vital public schemes designed to support people in times of unemployment or illness.

Education was a focal point of debate in many countries. In New Zealand, 4 out of 10 schools were said to have gone into deficit, in many cases because competition with neighbouring schools had resulted in the purchase of unnecessary equipment bought simply in order to out-do local rivals. *The Times* of India reported on a 'great overhaul' of the Indian education system, with authorities planning to turn schools into a 'fun-filled experience' in which 'students [...] want to come even when they are ill'. Elsewhere, however, there were reports of crisis in the Indian education system, with concerns that just 7% of the workforce were in secure, high-skill employment, in part because the vast majority of citizens did not continue their education beyond high-school level. Similarly, European Union (EU) leaders warned that the slow pace of educational reform in Europe might threaten the future competitiveness of the region's economy.

We found many such instances of social policy and economic policy concerns overlapping. There were reports that the scarcity of skills in the Chinese labour force is creating problems for foreign investment in China, for despite a vast pool of available employees, skills shortages are making it more and more difficult for foreign companies to fill job vacancies with suitably qualified candidates. In order to address its own national skills shortage, the Danish government announced that it intends to open new embassies around the globe to support foreign nationals who want to work in Denmark. In the UK, meanwhile, one of the smaller political parties demanded a five-year freeze on immigration on the grounds that it would 'ease pressure' on public services.

Housing pressures were also evident in many countries. The *Sydney Morning Herald* reported that housing shortages in Sydney, Australia, were causing year-on-year increases in housing costs in the city, threatening the affordability of homes and the stability of the local economy. In the UK, new figures showed that the average home in Britain cost five times the average first-time buyer's income. Prompted by house price pressures, furniture giant IKEA, together with a local council, launched a range of flat-pack, self-build houses to be sold to people on low incomes. In the US, meanwhile, the New York City government decided to help finance some new low-cost housing for teachers in an attempt to address the shortage of educators in the city. Elsewhere in the US, however, different housing-related issues were present. In San Diego, the city council vowed to adopt more stringent rules about grading and filling on hillsides after 75 homes had to be evacuated following a landslide. And in Tennessee, a local businessman killed himself with a gun after local politicians refused his request to reclassify his shop-house as a commercial premise.

All of these issues are matters of social policy. Social policy issues form the core of most domestic political debates and of some of the major international ones too. Social policies speak directly to the major concerns of our everyday lives: they shape our working lives, school lives and home lives and influence our living standards and living conditions. Social policies address the big questions of who gets what in society, why they should get it and how. It is precisely because social policies deal with these big issues that concern us all that it is such an interesting and important subject.

Yet it is also because social policies deal with such big issues that the question of how they might best be studied is open to such debate. Indeed, we can draw a distinction between social policy as a field of government action, and (the capitalised) Social Policy as a field of academic study. In terms of social policy, governments rarely concern themselves with definitional issues of what does or does not constitute a 'social' policy rather than, say, an 'economic' policy: they simply get on with the business of government in whichever way they see fit. In terms of Social Policy, however, there is a need to undertake such definitional work, even if only to determine what ought to be covered by textbooks and degree courses. Yet, because social policies cover such wide fields of action and because governments – and social problems – do not stand still, such a task is more difficult than it might appear at first sight. Furthermore, academics regularly reassess the core analytic tools and theories they use to understand issues and this, in turn, can lead to the boundaries of any subject also being redrawn.

The key pillars of social policy

The long debate among academics about the scope of social policy has led to a considerable widening of the subject in recent decades. While this extension of the subject is certainly to be welcomed, our aim here is to provide a *short introduction*. As such, we have taken a deliberate and considered decision to focus on a small number of fields of social policy, omitting discussion of many very interesting themes in order to make this concise. This, of course, raised a question for us as to which areas of social policy to cover in the book and what we offer here is something of a return to 'basics'.

In order to make sense of the complexity of social policy in practice, the main issues of policy are sometimes divided into subjects such as health, housing and employment. In the real world these fields of policy often overlap but in most countries there will be institutional structures

– government ministries, civil service departments, administrative offices and research units in universities – that divide reality into these specialist areas. In the traditional language of social policy these are sometimes referred to as the **pillars of welfare**. The idea of these issues as 'pillars' goes back to the foundation of the British welfare state in the 1940s as it emerged out of the traumatic events of the Second World War. When asked to review some elements of social policy in Britain during this period, the committee led by civil servant William Beveridge published a hugely influential report that provided a blueprint for a new social order in which poverty would become a thing of the past. Because the national state was responsible for the war effort it was to the state that people looked to put these promises into effect afterwards. Looking forward to the reconstruction of the UK after the war, the Beveridge Report (Beveridge, 1942) argued that there were 'five giants' that threatened the well-being of UK citizens in the post-war reconstruction process:

- **want** (an insufficient income);
- **idleness** (unemployment through insufficient job opportunities);
- **squalor** (poor housing conditions);
- **ignorance** (insufficient or poor-quality education); and
- **disease** (ill-health exacerbated by insufficient medical assistance).

These five giants map directly onto the five core pillars of welfare we examine in this book (see Table 1.1): **social security**, **employment**, **housing**, **education** and **health**. In the aftermath of the Second World War, the British government rapidly expanded and consolidated its activities in each of these areas in order to bring into being what is sometimes regarded as the first example of a 'welfare state' in Britain.

Because this is an introductory book we have decided to stick with this orthodox division partly for simplicity and partly because these institutional structures have, over the years, come to define the reality of modern welfare states. The institutions have taken on a life of their own. These five giants do not, however, cover the entirety of social policy provision. Indeed, other pillars of social policy play an essential role. For instance, it is often argued that there is another central pillar that, broadly speaking, revolves around social care. Some argue that

Table 1.1: From Beveridge's 'five giants' to modern-day pillars of welfare

Beveridge's giants	Key issues	Welfare pillars
Want	Insufficient income	Social security
Idleness	Lack of employment opportunities	Employment
Squalor	Poor-quality housing	Housing
Ignorance	Inadequate educational opportunities	Education
Disease	Limited access to healthcare	Health

policing and crime prevention are also part of the welfare state's pillars. It might be asked, therefore, why we have chosen to focus on the 'five giants' in this book. In part the answer is a pragmatic one: in order to deliver a short text we have, of course, had to omit many themes we find of interest. But in doing so, we asked ourselves what sorts of issues a student new to the subject would find most useful to see covered in such a book. Our conclusion was that, rather like a tourist guide, a good book should cover the main sights and sounds: while there will always be lots of very interesting sights hidden away from the main boulevards, the first-time visitor needs to grasp the basic layout of a city in order to orientate themselves in their new location. Our five pillars of welfare represent those main boulevards and each is considered in its own separate chapter.

Analysing social policy: concepts and theories

While our focus on the traditional pillars of welfare represents something of a return to basics, we would not, however, be content merely to repeat the time-worn approach to social policy found in the orthodox textbooks. In most of these, each chapter follows its own logic, with rather different social policy themes and issues being discussed under rather different headings. Typically, authors write from their own national perspective, with an historical overview of policy developments being presented along with a more detailed treatment of the most recent policy developments. In many ways this makes sense, for the different pillars of social policy do, indeed, deal with quite different social issues. Moreover, in some of the larger texts that deal with policy sectors, theories, ideologies and contextual issues, the sheer diversity of topics makes it difficult to adopt a common structure for each chapter. However, when setting out to write this book we thought that it ought to be possible in a short text to adopt a more systematic approach that bases each chapter around a common set of theoretically informed themes.

Our approach is based on using a common conceptual framework for each chapter that helps readers explore the differences and similarities between the 'pillars' and at the same time enables comparisons between countries rather than offering an overview of policy developments in just one nation. This allows much greater clarity and enables the real world to be understood and interpreted more easily. Indeed, one of the main problems of the orthodox versions of social policy is that they are often somewhat shy about engaging with social theory. We have no hesitation in introducing readers to social theory right at the outset of this book in the belief that this knowledge base is an essential tool, is simply understood and enables a quantum leap for students who can begin very quickly to read both the bigger story of social policy around the planet and to understand their own country and how it fits into the wider picture. Once again, as this is a short introduction to social policy, we cannot offer a comprehensive review of theoretical perspectives and have based our conceptual framework on a favoured piece of work.

In his classic text *The three worlds of welfare capitalism*, Esping-Andersen (1990) argued that there were different types of welfare systems around the world, with different ideologies and different principles underpinning social policy programmes in different countries. Indeed, as the title of his book suggests, he believed that there were three different types to be found in the high-income capitalist nations. This was an important observation, for it is sometimes presumed that because social policies are designed to address specific needs that are common to all nations (for example, housing policy addresses the universal need for housing), common policy solutions exist around the globe or that a consideration of the evidence will point to a common 'best way' forward. This is far from the case and Esping-Andersen argued that very different responses to common social pressures exist.

Crucially, Esping-Andersen's analysis was not based merely on analysis of facts and figures or descriptions of policy systems in each country he analysed. Instead, he drew on rich theoretical debates to help him identify what he suggested were the key features of national welfare systems. Indeed, his book began with a long section on social theory in which he explained his framework for comparing countries: without it he could make no sense of modern welfare systems and their many differences. On the basis of this review of social theory he highlighted three key dimensions of social policy on which he felt differences in approach could be identified across countries.

First, he argued that social policies were concerned with **social rights** in that they offered individuals protection against the fates that might befall them if they lived in a purely capitalist society in which the only means of generating income was through work. Here Esping-Andersen built on classic work such as Marshall's (1950) argument that the development of the welfare state represented the culmination of a long march of rights, providing citizens with important social rights alongside their legal and political rights (see Dwyer, 2004, for a discussion of social citizenship). It has long been observed that social policies are concerned with rights and the *Universal Declaration of Human Rights* states that all humans have a right to education and a 'standard of living adequate for [their] health and well-being' (UN General Assembly, 1948, Articles 25 and 26). However, there are many different ways in which these rights can be met and countries vary radically in terms of how extensively they support these social (and human) rights. So, when examining social policies, Esping-Andersen encouraged us to examine the varying strength and nature of these social rights. For instance, in some countries – such as the US – the state only provides healthcare to a minority of people. This means that some people, such as the young boy Deamonte Driver we mentioned at the start of this chapter, must rely on private services or miss out on treatment if they cannot afford it. In other countries, such as Sweden, however, the state provides healthcare to all citizens. While both countries operate healthcare systems for citizens, the extent of these systems varies radically. Or, in other words, the strength of the social right to healthcare differs.

Building on this question of the nature of social rights, Esping-Andersen argued that varying social rights hinted at broad differences in how societies respond to core social needs. More specifically, he felt there were key differences in terms of the balance of responsibilities faced by the state, the market, the community and families or individuals. For instance, as in our example above, in some societies the state might play a dominant role in providing healthcare services, but in others it might be the private market that does so. In other words, Esping-Andersen encouraged us to examine how social policies are organised in different countries. Again, he drew on classic work in the field of social policy. Titmuss (1956) famously argued that it was possible to observe a social division of welfare, with welfare being provided not through state services but via the tax system and by employers. More recently, theorists have used terms such as **welfare pluralism** (see Johnson, 1987) or the **mixed economy of welfare** (see Powell, 2007) to capture the idea that welfare is provided not just by the state but also by private companies, by voluntary organisations and, indeed, by families and communities. Esping-Andersen felt that differences between nations in how far they relied on, say, public or private services to meet welfare needs, told us a great deal about the nature of their social policies, so he placed this notion of a 'mixed economy of welfare' at the heart of his exploration of social policies.

Finally, and following on from the previous two issues, Esping-Andersen suggested that differing social rights and responsibilities had a clear impact on the distribution of resources in societies. For example, a largely privately based system of healthcare might result in richer citizens having better access to services while a state-based system might provide more equal access. Esping-Andersen suggested that all social policies impact on the **stratification** of society and encouraged us to examine their impact on the distribution of resources and opportunities. Again he echoed a long tradition of work in the social sciences, not least classic early pieces of sociology such as Tawney's (1931) *Equality*.

These three issues provide the core themes for each chapter in our book. We have not employed them in strictly the same way as Esping-Andersen did – not least because he only really examined social security in *The three worlds of welfare capitalism* – but they provide the foundation for our approach. Indeed, to simplify matters, we have interpreted the issues in a slightly looser manner, although still following his threefold division of the issues.

First, each chapter of the book begins by asking what are the *key policy goals* that policy might address in each pillar. Thus the first section of each chapter asks: what might policy aim to do? The crucial point here is that, in practice, the policy goals can differ from country to country, so we offer a flavour of the different types of approach that might exist in each sector. Often these differing policy goals are rooted in different ideologies or different sets of values.

Understanding that policy can have different goals is an important starting point for thinking through how each pillar of welfare might be organised. Indeed, because different countries often try to address different policy goals in each pillar, we often see quite different healthcare, housing and education systems around the world. To demonstrate this, the second section of each chapter explores the *key delivery mechanisms* that might be used in each pillar. It asks: how might services be organised? To echo a point made above, it is important to stress that there is no single best approach in each pillar. Instead, there are different policy instruments that have different advantages and disadvantages. In this section we outline the main policy tools along with some of the main pros and cons of each.

This hints at the fact that policy making is often a difficult balancing act: different policy mechanisms will advantage and disadvantage different groups of people and reconciling competing interests is far from easy. The third and final core section of each chapter examines the *key policy issues* in each pillar. It asks: who is/is not benefiting from the services delivered in each pillar? In so doing, it aims to examine how policy ameliorates or reinforces social divisions and social inequalities.

Table 1.2 summarises the ways in which Esping-Andersen's framework maps onto ours; while different issues will necessarily be raised in each chapter, each will be organised under the headings in the right-hand column of this table.

Table 1.2: From Esping-Andersen's themes to our headings		
Esping-Andersen's themes	**Key issues**	**Our heading**
Social rights	What is provided?	Key policy goals
State, market, family	How is it provided?	Key delivery mechanisms
Stratification	Who benefits?	Key policy issues

Adopting an international focus

One of the strengths of Esping-Andersen's definition of the core features of social policy is that it can draw attention to different approaches to the provision of welfare in different countries. As well as focusing on the traditional pillars of welfare and examining each through a common set of themes, the third dimension of the approach we have adopted in this book is that it has an international focus. Because our book is written in a thematic fashion we feel that this divorces it from the specifics of a particular national case. As we noted above, in most social policy textbooks, the individual chapters on health, employment, social security and so on are based around a lengthy consideration of practice in the author's own nation. We will instead draw on examples from around the world when exploring the key policy goals, mechanisms and issues in each pillar of welfare.

From an intellectual viewpoint, we feel that the focus on one national case unnecessarily constrains discussion of social policies: if we are to understand the possibilities of social policy in practice then it makes sense to reflect on a wider range of national experiences, not least because the differences between nations can often be quite stark. We have tried here to include examples from a wide range of countries, although data limitations (and, indeed, our own intellectual limitations) mean that there is a bias towards the more heavily researched high-income countries. (The World Bank classifies countries on the basis of their national income per capita [that is, per person]. In 2007, countries with a national income of US$11,116 per person or above were classified as being high-income countries.) Crucially, although there are biases towards some countries that we are more familiar with, no single country provides the basis of the discussion in our chapters. Indeed, we draw on examples from every populated continent of the world and cite examples and evidence from more than 70 countries.

However, we should again stress that our book is merely a short guide; while we will draw on examples from many different countries we do not aim to provide a comprehensive overview of how nations differ or detailed descriptions of welfare arrangements in different countries. Those readers who wish to gain deeper knowledge of this sort should consult one of the many excellent comparative social policy textbooks that are available.

Conclusion

It is hoped that the core features of our approach will now be clear:

- a brief overview of the five core pillars of social policy, each examined individually in their own chapter;
- three conceptually rooted themes providing a common structure for each chapter;
- an international approach that is not rooted in the example of one nation.

In order to meet these goals, we have adopted a particular style of writing that is worth us briefly explaining here.

Each chapter has a relatively short narrative that examines the key issues under our headings of 'key policy goals', 'key delivery mechanisms' and 'key policy issues'. The narrative aims to explain key terms (which are displayed in bold) and outline the key issues and debates. Examples are kept to a minimum, as are references to other sources. Accompanying the narrative are text boxes and figures that offer greater detail. Sometimes the text boxes and figures offer a case study of one or two nations, sometimes they explore a key debate or concept in more depth and sometimes they offer useful data or charts. Finally, we draw each chapter to a close by offering a *summary* and a *reading guide*. The latter is particularly important for we must stress that the aim of this book is merely to provide an *introduction*. To use the guide book analogy once again, while we explore the key features of the main boulevards here, there are so many interesting 'hidden side streets' and 'secret suburbs' that we would encourage you to explore further once you have orientated yourself during your initial visit. Our guide to further reading aims to point you towards the gems of the city that are off the main tourist track described here.

2
social security

Introduction

Social security is at the heart of the welfare state, but its precise meaning is difficult to pin down for it often means quite different things in different countries. This is even true of countries that share the same language – such as the UK and US – and reflects the very different historical, political and cultural underpinnings of social policies across the world. Given this, the use of the terms 'income protection' or 'social protection' is sometimes preferred in place of 'social security', for the principal goal of the policies we describe in this chapter is to provide financial support to people whose income is threatened by common events that might, for instance, make it difficult for them to generate sufficient income through paid employment.

The following contingencies, risks and needs are typically covered by 'social security':

- unemployment
- old age and widow(er)hood
- sickness
- disability
- employment injury and occupational disease
- raising children
- maternity/paternity leave.

A wider definition of 'social security' also includes help with housing costs (see Chapter Six), basic education (see Chapter Four) and a general scheme of financial support for those deemed to have an insufficient income (often called 'social assistance').

The scale and importance of social security schemes can be illustrated by pointing to their cost (see Table 2.1). In high-income countries these schemes typically account for between 10% and 20% of Gross Domestic Product (GDP), although countries with the most comprehensive systems sometime spend as much as 25%. The sums of money involved are often mind-boggling as a consequence: the UK spends well in excess of US$200 billion annually. Poorer countries tend to have less comprehensive schemes of support. In upper middle-income countries expenditure of 5%-10% of GDP is not uncommon, but in lower middle-income countries and low-income countries social security often accounts for just 1% or 2% of GDP. (The World Bank classifies countries on the basis of their national income per capita [that is, per person]. In 2007, countries with a national income of US$905 per person or less were classified as being low-income countries.) In some of the poorest countries there is no real system of social security as it is conventionally understood with financial support coming mainly from the family, the local community, benefits attached to employment or, in some cases, personal appeals to the beneficence of local rulers. However, while richer countries tend to spend more, there is no strictly deterministic link between a nation's wealth and the comprehensiveness of its social security system. As Table 2.1 shows, there are places with high incomes but low spending – such as Hong Kong – and low-income countries or lower-middle-income countries such as Iran and Mongolia that devote relatively large proportions of their GDP to social security.

Key policy goals

At the most basic level, the goal of social security can be defined as protecting the income of individuals or families in the face of common contingencies or risks such as old age or unemployment. To do this, welfare states commonly put in place a series of social security programmes such as pensions, unemployment benefits, child or family benefits, sickness benefits and maternity/paternity benefits. In each case,

Table 2.1: Social security expenditure (as % of GDP), 2003	
High-income countries	
Sweden	24.9
Netherlands	18.4
United Kingdom	16.2
Hong Kong, China (SAR)	2.8
Upper middle-income countries	
Russian Federation	10.5
Mauritius	5.2
Costa Rica	4.2
Lower middle-income countries	
Iran (Islamic Republic of)	7.2
Lesotho	1.7
Maldives	1.6
El Salvador	0.3
Low-income countries	
Mongolia	7.9
Vietnam	2.7
Bhutan	0.0

Sources: Computed from World Bank (2007) and IMF (2007a, 2007b) figures. World Bank country classifications

the programme is based primarily around **cash transfers** from the state to individuals, but sometimes also includes **benefits-in-kind** (see Box 2.2 later in this chapter).

However, this relatively simple view of social security masks a much more complex set of goals in reality. **Income protection** may be the core ostensible goal, but there are considerable variations across the high-income countries in terms of which contingencies are protected against, when they are covered, who is entitled to support and the generosity of the benefit payments. For instance, in the US a long-term unemployed single man with no dependants would be entitled to very little support from the state; in 2004, such a man who had previously been employed on average wages would have received social security benefits equivalent to a mere 7% of the pay packet he had previously taken home (OECD, 2006a). By contrast, someone in the same situation in Sweden would have received 52% of his previous salary. Similarly, a man on average earnings who retired in 2005 would have had 53% of his income replaced by the state pension scheme in Norway, but a similar man in New Zealand would have had just 38% of his income replaced (OECD, 2005a).

What these figures indicate is that in making decisions about the seemingly technical issue of 'income protection', governments must also tackle deeply *moral and political questions* about who gets what, when and why. The differences in support for the long-term unemployed in Sweden and the US are stark on paper, and may seem hard to justify, but they reflect differing judgements on how long it is reasonable for the state to support someone without employment who is looking for work. In the short term, the differences in payment levels between these two countries are not so great: 77% and 62% of average earnings are replaced by the schemes in Sweden and the US respectively (OECD, 2006a). What this demonstrates is that the system in the US is designed around the presumption that an individual may need short-term support when they lose a job, but that after a given period – usually six months – they should be able to find re-employment. The Swedish system, however, reflects quite a different view – that structural weaknesses in the economy may sometimes make it difficult for an individual to find appropriate employment. Consequently, their 'short-term' support lasts for 60 weeks and is supplemented by a fairly generous form of longer-term support after this (see also Scruggs, 2005). In other words, the two systems differ in terms of how they look to balance a citizen's *rights* to income protection with their *responsibilities* to secure an income through work (see Chapter Three).

Each branch of social security has its own unique policy issues. While a key tension in designing unemployment benefits lies in balancing income protection and stimulating prompt re-entry into the labour market, schemes that supplement the income of those unable to work due to ill-health have to tackle the thorny issue of deciding when someone is too ill to work, and pensions programmes have to make clear when someone is entitled to retire. However, what all social security schemes have in common is that they *redistribute income* within society: from rich to poor, from generation to generation, from those without children to those with children and so on. Given their cost, social security schemes require substantial contributions from taxpayers and businesses in order to finance payments, but how far societies are willing to support the redistribution of income varies considerably.

In his classic study *The three worlds of welfare capitalism*, Esping-Andersen (1990) analysed the protection offered by pensions, unemployment insurance and sickness insurance in 18 high-income countries and argued that their welfare states broke into three distinct types, largely on the basis of the strength of their social protection and their redistributional intent:

■ *The liberal regime:* offers low levels of income protection that often do not stretch beyond providing a basic safety net and little redistribution of income, meaning that the levels of inequality generated by the market largely remain.
■ *The social democratic regime:* offers high levels of income protection and income is redistributed between social groups with the aim of creating a more equal society.
■ *The conservative/corporatist regime:* offers high levels of income protection, but there is only a modest redistribution of income between social classes – social security acts as a savings bank to protect against common risks rather than as a tool for promoting greater equality.

In other words, Esping-Andersen found significant differences between countries in terms of policy goals. Crucially, he argued that these variations represented long-term historical differences between nations in terms of the choices they have made about their social security systems.

Key delivery mechanisms

The variations Esping-Andersen (1990) identifies are not just about different levels of spending on particular benefits or different rates of payment to benefit recipients. Just as important are the different delivery mechanisms that are deployed, for while all social security programmes transfer cash payments, the ways in which these payments are organised have a huge impact on the type of support benefit recipients receive. Indeed, the delivery mechanisms that underpin social security programmes often act to institutionalise their core principles.

First and foremost, social security programmes differ in how they determine who is entitled to receive payments. There are essentially three core approaches here: benefits can be universal, means tested or insurance based. When benefits are **universal**, all citizens who meet the relevant contingency receive a payment; the UK's universal Child Benefit, for instance, is paid to all families with children. By contrast, a **means-tested** benefit will only go to those citizens who, when faced with the relevant contingency, are living below a specified income level. In Australia in 2004, for example, anyone out of work with an income of more than AUS$586 per fortnight (through, say, property investments) would not be entitled to any payment from the country's main benefit for the unemployed (the New Start Allowance) (OECD, 2006a). Finally, **social insurance** benefits are based on the **contribution principle**: in order to claim a particular benefit when faced with the relevant contingency a citizen needs to have made a specified number of contributions to the insurance fund. In Germany, for instance, unemployment insurance benefits can only be claimed by those who have made contributions to the fund for at least 12 months in the previous three years – those who do not meet this level have to rely on the less generous social assistance safety net (OECD, 2006a).

In terms of determining benefit payment levels (see Box 2.1), a distinction is commonly drawn between earnings-related and flat-rate benefits. **Earnings-related benefits** provide citizens with a cash transfer that equates to a proportion of the income they received from employment before they became sick, unemployed or retired and so on. What this means in practice is that benefit payments will vary from person to person: in Sweden, unemployment insurance is calculated at 80% of previous earnings (subject to a maximum ceiling), so a woman who had earned SEK750,000 as a doctor would receive cash transfers that were substantially higher than a man who had worked as a sales assistant with a salary of SEK100,000 per year (OECD, 2006a). When benefits are **flat-rate**, however, the same level of payment goes to all irrespective of their prior income. This is the case with unemployment benefit in New Zealand where, for example, in 2004 all single people aged 25 or over were (subject to passing a means test) paid NZ$193.92 per week, irrespective of their former income (OECD, 2006a).

Box 2.1	Determining social security benefit rates

In providing a system of 'income protection' for citizens, all social security systems create a de facto 'social minimum' – a level of income the state believes no one should fall below. In addition, policy makers also need to decide which benefits should pay at this level and which should pay above it.

For earnings-related insurance benefits these decisions are heavily influenced by contribution rates: indeed, they often operate on a **defined benefit** basis – in exchange for contributions of a certain percentage of income they guarantee payments of a certain level of income. However, with flat-rate and means-tested benefits there is no link to prior income, so the rates they are paid at tend to be more heavily influenced by political considerations about what is affordable. This is particularly so with regard to social assistance benefits that form the last-resort safety net. Some countries – such as South Korea – try to adopt a technical approach to determining payment levels by creating an *official minimum living standard* that is reassessed each year through an analysis of the cost of essential goods and services. This, however, merely raises the question of what are deemed essential goods and services. In many other countries, the social assistance net was initially based on similar sorts of considerations, but rates have been adjusted yearly without reassessing the precise costs of living they are supposed to cover.

Indeed, with the exception of the small number of benefits with payment levels tied to an annual reassessment of living standards, all benefits – that is, both flat-rate and earnings-related – need to be **uprated** each year to account for changing living standards. Broadly speaking, there are two key approaches here. The first is to uprate benefits in line with *inflation*: this accounts for the annual change in the cost of goods and services. However, adopting this approach means that benefits risk falling behind the more general growth in living standards, because wages tend to grow at a faster rate than inflation. A more generous approach, therefore, is to uprate benefits in line with *earnings*. There is also a third approach that is often used: uprating as a political act. At the risk of appearing cynical, it is not all that uncommon in some countries for unusually generous additional increases to be made to some benefits in advance of a general election.

It is often the case that insurance-based benefits are paid on an earnings-related basis and means-tested benefits on a flat-rate basis. This is because the way these benefits are typically financed heavily influences their payment processes. Insurance-based benefits are tied to the contributions made by individuals, often with matching contributions from their employer. As such, benefits of this form can be viewed as social insurance and are not unlike insurance payments that an individual might pay to cover other risks: against their car being damaged in an accident or valuable items being stolen from their home. Social insurance contributions are often fixed as a certain percentage of income – at the time of writing German citizens had to pay 9.95% of their income into pension insurance, for instance. This means that higher earners pay more into social insurance funds than low earners and it is on this basis that higher payments to higher earners are justified: in principle there is a direct – actuarial – link between contributions to a fund and the payments that can be received from it. By contrast, means-tested benefits are typically used when the state wants to target payments at the poorest in society (sometimes means-tested benefits are dubbed 'selective' – as opposed to universal – benefits because of this) and are normally financed through general taxation. Here, entitlement is not based on contribution but on demonstrated need and payments are not tied to previous income but designed to boost incomes that are seen as insufficient. In other words, means-tested benefits tend to have flat-rate, rather than earnings-related, payments. However, it is important to note that this is not always so: there are instances of flat-rate-based social insurance benefits (the UK's unemployment insurance benefit – known as Jobseeker's Allowance – for instance) and many means-tested benefits offer variable payment levels depending on a claimant's circumstances (South Korea, for example, has a means-tested social assistance safety net that pays the difference between a household's income and a legally defined minimum cost of living). Moreover, many insurance schemes that appear to be actuarial are, in practice, funded through general taxation with insurance contributions simply going into the government's coffers rather than into a ring-fenced fund.

In practice, social security programmes almost always involve a mix of the above benefit types. Indeed, it is common for there to be a more generous insurance-based benefit that provides cover for insured employees, which is supplemented by a less generous means-tested safety net for those who are not insured. Added to this, it is often the case that entitlement to the insurance-based benefit is time limited – we have already noted that unemployment insurance in the US is limited to the first six months of unemployment, for example – and claimants have to move to a means-tested benefit after this time. In some countries, even access to the means-tested safety net is time limited (see Box 2.2). Many countries also stipulate waiting periods before payments are made: in Iceland, for instance, a claim for unemployment insurance is not payable for the first seven days of unemployment. Generally speaking, the rules and restrictions attached to benefits claims tend to be stricter for those deemed able to work; indeed, one of the trends witnessed in recent years has been the increased *conditionality* of payments to those of working age as an attempt to link work and welfare more closely (see Chapter Three). This is true both for those who are unemployed – who increasingly have to demonstrate the efforts they are making to find re-employment – and for those who are sick or disabled – who are being increasingly asked to prove that their condition is severe enough to prevent them from working.

Box 2.2	The 'social security' and 'welfare' division in the US

While in most countries the term 'social security' is used to refer to cash transfer programmes as a whole, in the US it refers only to the social insurance programmes that exist for older people, disabled people and survivors (widow[er]s). These contribution-based benefits are administered by a federal (that is, national) agency – Social Security Administration – and they operate on an earnings-related basis and make relatively generous payments.

The core non-insurance cash transfer programmes, however, are termed 'welfare' and operate on a very different basis. Chief among these is Temporary Assistance for Needy Families (TANF), which is mainly funded by the federal government but is administered by each of the 50 states in the US. The precise details can vary from state to state as a consequence, but the key principles do not: TANF is a means-tested programme that acts as a minimal safety net, paying very modest sums of money to low-income families. In addition, support is very strictly time limited, with the national rules allowing for no more than five years of support over a person's lifetime. In some states the maximum period of support is less than this.

The second main plank of 'welfare' in the US comes in the form of the food stamps programme. While social security programmes are mostly based around cash transfers, sometime benefits-in-kind also form part of the provision. Like TANF, food stamps are funded by the federal government but administered by the states. As the name implies, food stamps are vouchers or cheques (and, increasingly, electronic accounts) that recipients use to purchase food. They form a substantial part of the welfare package in the US – replacing support that would come as cash in many countries – and the ostensible aim is to promote high levels of nutrition among low-income families.

In other words, the separation of social protection into 'social security' and 'welfare' in the US can be seen not just in the language used, but also in the level and structure of payments, the bodies that administer payments, the length of entitlements and even the form in which payments are made. All of these factors serve to emphasise the difference between recipients of the two sets of programmes: while social security recipients are painted as 'deserving' cases, welfare recipients are often portrayed as 'undeserving' and 'welfare dependants', particularly by the conservative 'moral majority'.

These populist divisions play heavily on common stereotypes about which groups are 'hardworking' or 'deserving'. In truth, these stereotypes reflect who has the most political power in the US. Lone parents and African Americans have borne the brunt of recent welfare reforms – because they are disproportionately over-represented among North America's poor and under-represented among its political class. Meanwhile, social security – in which middle-class and white North Americans are over-represented – has escaped significant cutbacks over the same period.

How, then, do the differing mechanisms for the delivery of social security relate to the differing goals of social security we highlighted above? Esping-Andersen (1990) suggested the following:

■ *The liberal regime:* strong reliance on means-tested benefits that provide a basic safety net through flat-rate payments.
■ *The social democratic regime:* emphasis on generous universal benefits that provide a comprehensive system of social protection.
■ *The conservative/corporatist regime:* social insurance benefits predominate, providing a strong system of social protection, but heavy use of earnings-related benefits mutes the redistributive impact.

While our emphasis here has been on income protection administered by the state, we should add – following Esping-Andersen again – that the state is far from the only provider of income support (see Box 2.3). In many societies, privately financed and operated schemes – such as pensions or sickness insurance – play a major role in fact. In Canada, the Netherlands and the US around one third of pensions-related spending is privately based and in Australia it is almost half (Adema and Ladaique, 2005). Likewise, 'cash transfers' between family members are hugely significant in many countries, particularly those where family obligations are very firmly culturally embedded. The voluntary sector also plays a role in some countries through organisations such as friendly societies that organise pooled savings schemes on a not-for-profit basis.

Box 2.3	**Income protection beyond the state**

The state is by no means the only provider of income protection. In most countries there are extensive private programmes, particularly in the field of pensions. Indeed, it is very common for pension provisions to be linked to employment in a particular field: so-called 'occupational pensions' that, for instance, might cater for all school teachers in a country. Similarly, in many countries it is common for individuals to save money in a personal private pension managed by profit-making financial institutions. However, the state usually plays a key role in either encouraging such private programmes (through tax breaks on contributions, for instance) or discouraging them (by providing an extensive public system that negates the need for additional support, for example); its role is rarely neutral. Moreover, it should also be noted that private social spending tends to favour the rich more than the poor for it caters only for those who can afford to pay into schemes.

In some countries the not-for-profit sector plays an important role in social security provision. In Sweden, for example, unemployment insurance is administered by a range of unemployment insurance societies that, for the most part, are organised and managed by trade unions, albeit with the state playing a key role in so far as it both endorses the system and makes financial contributions towards it. Religious bodies also play a significant role in some countries. In Italy, for instance, the absence of a national social assistance scheme means that provision is patchy in some regions and/or for some groups (especially migrants) and the Catholic Church operates schemes in many places that provide a mixture of benefits-in-kind alongside some benefits-in-cash.

Families play a key role too. While for most people families are a natural source of support in times of need, the extent of their role is often heavily influenced by the formal rules of social security systems. For example, in Taiwan, the means test for claimants of social assistance includes not only the financial resources of the claimant – deemed as any income from work, property and investments, plus savings and property assets – but also the same resources held by the claimant's spouse, their parents and children (whether living with the claimant or not) and, if in the same household, the resources of the claimant's siblings too. One consequence of this strict means test is that few people are deemed poor enough for assistance: just 0.4% of the population in 2004 (Fu, 2006). In the absence of state support, of course, assistance from family becomes all the more important.

Key policy issues

While social security, concerned as it is with applying rules and transferring monies, is a technical and somewhat bureaucratic field of social policy, it should also be clear by now that the rules embedded within social security systems are of enormous significance because of the impact they have on the strength of social rights, on the distribution of income within society and, more generally, on employment. It is precisely because of this – allied with the huge sums of money involved – that social security can be such a contentious area of policy. Indeed, it is a field where policy makers are faced with some huge policy issues.

If the chief goal of social security programmes is to protect incomes, then we might expect well-functioning systems to eliminate **poverty**. Yet, the truth is that there is no social security system anywhere in the world that manages to do this completely. Much depends on how we define poverty, an issue over which there is much debate, but Figure 2.1 displays poverty rates in 24 of the richest countries in the world using one of the standard measures used in high-income countries: the percentage of individuals living below 50% of median income. It highlights strong variations between countries with high poverty rates in, for example, the US and Ireland (17.1% and 15.4% in poverty respectively) and more modest levels of poverty in, for example, Sweden and Denmark (5.3%

Figure 2.1: Social protection spending and poverty, 2000

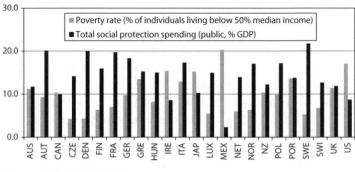

Source: OECD (2006b, 2007a)

and 4.3% respectively). Alongside the bars showing the poverty rate in these nations are bars showing the proportion of GDP each country spends on cash transfers: there is, unsurprisingly perhaps, a strong link between the two, countries with lower poverty rates generally being those with more extensive social security systems.

However, evidence of a link between comprehensive social protection and low poverty rates is not enough to persuade many decision makers that an extensive social security system is a necessary investment. As we have hinted throughout, this is in large part a consequence of the substantial level of spending – and therefore taxation – such a system requires. Added to this are commonplace worries in many countries that increased life expectancy and diminishing birthrates are creating a *demographic time bomb*: fewer future workers to support greater numbers of future pensioners will make systems still more expensive to future taxpayers. Much of the debate about social security in recent years has surrounded the impact large expenditures have on economic performance. The chief arguments include suggestions that high levels of taxation deter business from investing in the economy and that requiring employers to contribute to social insurance funds makes them less willing to employ people. There is a vocal school of thought which claims globalisation has heightened these dilemmas because businesses can move their investment from country to country much more easily than in the past. It has also been claimed that generous social security benefits can act as a disincentive to finding work and, consequently, foster **welfare dependency**. We will explore some of these issues in more detail in Chapter Three.

While there is no clear evidence of a link between strong social protection and weakened economic performance – far from it, in fact – many politicians have been keen to at least restrict the growth of social security spending in recent years. One of the ways in which this has often occurred is through greater reliance on means-tested benefits. While the increased targeting that is associated with these benefits can appeal to policy makers keen to get maximum value for money – because cash is focused on the poorest – means-tested benefits carry some inherent problems. Chief among these is the issue of *take-up*. Means-tested benefits typically have lower rates of take-up than universal benefits: many of those who are entitled to claim them do not. There are many reasons for this – including the fact that they are not paid automatically after a particular event (such as retirement) but, instead, have to be actively claimed – but it is often suggested that there is more *stigma* attached to means-tested benefits than those that are universal or insurance based. In part this is because claiming them requires an individual to demonstrate that they are poor by providing a great deal of personal and financial information to support their claim. But on top of this, while universal benefits can be clearly seen as a *social right of citizenship* – because they are paid to all citizens – and entitlement to insurance-based benefits is clearly earned through the payment of contributions, means-tested benefits are often perceived as an *unearned payment*, *charity* or a *hand-out*, making some people reluctant to claim them. In some countries the distinction between means-tested and insurance-based benefits is heavily underlined by the fact that they are administered by separate bodies, institutionalising a commonly held view that there is a division between **deserving** and **undeserving** claimants (see Box 2.2).

Another problem that arises with means tests is that of defining the *threshold* against which means are tested. Determining where to draw the line between an income that is deemed sufficient and one that is deemed insufficient is difficult to say the least (see Box 2.1). Moreover, in drawing such a line, there is a danger that **poverty traps** are created when a citizen in receipt of a means-tested benefit can actually see their income drop if increased earnings from employment lead to the withdrawal of their benefits. On top of this, means tests are often assessed against savings and assets as well as income. In such cases, the aim is to rule out claims from those with substantial amounts of money stored in the bank. While this may seem logical if a benefit is aimed at the poorest, it is often argued that such rules create *perverse incentives* because they penalise those who have saved money for a rainy day. An even thornier issue is that of whose income to assess. Often it is a family's income that counts rather than simply an individual's, but defining what counts as 'family' can often be a complex task and there are some marked variations across countries. While most equate family with household, there are countries where a family with children making a claim for support will find that the incomes of the children's grandparents and even aunties and uncles will be taken into account when assessing claims for support (see Box 2.3).

Yet, while there are clear problems in utilising means-tested benefits, there are also problems that arise from heavy use of insurance-based benefits too. Chief among these is the fact that they exclude those with a weak contribution record or without one at all because of infrequent or patchy employment. This can be a particular problem for people who have spent considerable periods of time outside of the labour market while caring for family members. Because women are more likely to undertake such caring responsibilities in practice, many insurance-based benefits – particularly pension schemes – disadvantage women by failing to account for unpaid work when totting up 'contributions'. While universal benefits do not in principle exclude anyone, and should avoid this particular problem, once again the reality does not always meet the theory. While universal benefits are paid as a social right of citizenship, most societies contain a not insubstantial number of inhabitants who do not have full citizenship status. In particular, migrant workers and asylum seekers are often denied access to key social security benefits that are ostensibly universal.

Indeed, because access to social security – or the terms on which it is offered – often favours some social groups over others, it is important to look beneath the headline figures on poverty shown in Figure 2.1, for they can mask some of the more subtle social divisions. One of the more prominent trends in high-income countries is the much higher rates of poverty that we see in lone-parent households when compared to households generally, as shown in Figure 2.2. Again, however, there are important differences between countries. Some work hard to reduce poverty in single-parent households through the social security system. In 2004, Denmark, for instance, paid all lone parents DKK4,228 per year on top of normal family allowances and another DKK4,156 per child per year – and more still if the absent parent did not make any contributions to household income (OECD, 2006a). Other nations, however, often penalise lone-parent households, either by providing very

Figure 2.2: Poverty^a and family type, 1999/2000

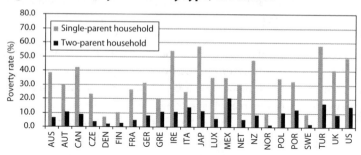

Note: ^a Poverty as households living below 50% median income

Source: OECD (2006b)

low rates of support or, in some cases, by favouring married couples in the taxation system.

What all this suggests is that, far from being 'merely' concerned with protecting incomes, social security rules are heavily shaped by power relations in society. While it is beyond the scope of this book to explore this issue, we might reflect on it by noting that despite displaying the highest levels of poverty in most high-income societies, lone-parent households are the group that has been most consistently targeted by politicians looking to restrict social security entitlements in recent years. This in turn hints at another important feature of social security systems that is often overlooked: they are well used by the *rich as well as the poor*. While it is often presumed that the bulk of social security spending goes to the poorest or most vulnerable and marginalised groups in society, this is not the case in practice. In the year 2000, the poorest 30% of working-age households received only a marginally greater share of income transfers than the richest 30% in Germany and France, while in Italy and Portugal the richest 30% actually received more than twice as much as the poorest 30% (OECD, 2005b).

SUMMARY

- ■ Social security is concerned with providing **income protection**.
- ■ Social security guards against **common risks** and **contingencies** such as unemployment and old age.
- ■ It does this primarily through **cash transfers**.
- ■ Social security takes many different forms including **means-tested**, **universal** and **insurance-based** benefits.
- ■ Payment rates vary substantially and can be **earnings-related** or **flat-rate**.
- ■ Social security has a huge impact on **poverty** and **inequality** in societies.
- ■ Social security is usually viewed as a government activity, but the private and voluntary sectors also play a key role, as do families.
- ■ Social security caters for rich and poor.
- ■ Social security embodies deeply moralistic principles.

READING GUIDE

Good overviews of social security are provided by Ditch (1999) and Millar (2003). Henman and Fenger (2006) provide a good review of recent welfare reform strategies around the world that pays particular attention to delivery issues on the ground. Clasen (1997) offers a useful, if a little dated, review of social insurance schemes around Europe and Saraceno (2002) provides a similarly useful review of social assistance safety nets. To find out more about the financing of social security, see Glennerster (2003). Ridge and Wright (2008) offer a good review of the interactions between social security and poverty, income and wealth. Froggett (2002) and Chan and Bowpitt (2005) offer interesting overviews of the emotive, moral and ethical issues that social security confronts. Similarly, Walker and Howard (2000) examine the claims that a 'welfare dependency culture' has emerged.

The Organisation for Economic Co-operation and Development (OECD) provides much easily accessible information about social protection arrangements in the high-income countries on its website at www.oecd.org. Two particularly useful publications it issues are *Benefits and wages* (OECD, 2006a) and *Society at a glance* (OECD, 2005b, 2006b).

Those interested in a more detailed account of national features of social security should also consider the US Social Security Administration's webpage on 'Social security programs throughout the world' (www.ssa. gov/policy/docs/progdesc/ssptw/), which provides concise information on coverage, qualifying conditions and benefit levels as well as the financing of the main social security programmes in 170 countries all over the world (SSA, 2007).

The Mutual Information System on Social Protection in the member states of the EU (MISSOC) is smaller in scope (http://ec.europa.eu/employment_ social/social_protection/index_en.htm); therefore the information provided is slightly more detailed and more strongly embedded in social policy discussions at the European level (MISSOC, 2007).

Students of comparative and international social policy will find that the field has been somewhat dominated by the analysis of social security. This has – at least partly – been influenced by the fact that macro-level spending data for social security have often been more readily available than, for instance, more complicated figures on actual benefit payments or take-up. It is again the OECD that has delivered the most comprehensive and most widely used statistics on social security spending in its *Social Expenditure Database* (OECD, 2007a). While the IMF's (2007b) *Government Finance Statistics* have become an alternative to the OECD's social security spending data in recent years – as it includes a much larger set of countries – access is not free of charge and thus often only feasible through university libraries.

The Asian Development Bank (2007) has taken big strides to make available key statistics on social and welfare issues including social inequality, unemployment and social security spending (www.adb.org/). It has become a valuable point of reference for students interested in this particular region of the world.

3

employment

Introduction

In Chapter Two we stressed that the precise definition and classification of social security schemes is a difficult endeavour. This is also certainly true for employment policies too. A *narrow* definition of the term typically separates so-called **passive** or reactive labour market programmes from **active** ones. Simply put, passive programmes look to provide income protection (see Chapter Two) for those without work, while active programmes aim to help those without work to find re-employment. The most common example of a passive employment policy is the payment of unemployment benefit. As we will discuss in this chapter, such policies have come to be viewed in an increasingly negative light, with many arguing that they are detrimental to the cause of solving the most severe labour market problems.

The OECD identifies five main types of active employment programmes (OECD, 2007b):

- First, there are *employment services*. While the precise nature of these services varies from country to country, public employment agencies or job centres are typically responsible for placing unemployed people into the labour market by matching them with job vacancies and providing advice on work opportunities. They often also administer payments of unemployment benefits and allocate jobless people to available slots in other labour market programmes such as training schemes.

- Second, *labour market training* can be offered to unemployed people in the form of vocational training or academic training and is sometimes offered to the already employed to help ensure their future employability in changing labour markets.
- Third, in many countries, there are specific *youth programmes* that either target young unemployed people or offer apprenticeships or craft training for young school leavers.
- Sometimes these tie in with a fourth approach, which is *subsidised employment*. In some countries, subsidies are paid to private sector companies in order to encourage the hiring of unemployed people. Typically these schemes contribute to a firm's wages costs if they agree to employ someone who has been out of work for a long period of time. Sometimes these subsidies can also be paid directly to unemployed people by granting financial support if they wish to start their own business. Furthermore, governments can create jobs directly in the public sector or in non-profit organisations too.
- Fifth, the OECD also points to specific *measures for disabled people*. Although this is a somewhat crude classification, it is intended to highlight the special vocational training programmes and sheltered employment programmes that many countries use to increase the employment rates of disabled people.

On average, spending for all of the above active labour market programmes accounted for 0.6% of GDP across the OECD in 2003, with the highest spenders in the OECD allocating between 1% and 1.5% of their GDP on activation policies, while the lowest spenders merely reached 0.1% of GDP (see Table 3.1).

Another way to look at the scale and importance of active labour market programmes is to relate them to expenditure on passive unemployment benefit payments. Only a few OECD countries spend more on active than on passive labour market measures (see also Table 3.1). Indeed, most countries spend around twice as much on unemployment benefits as they do on active labour market programmes.

This *narrow* definition of employment policy as a trade-off between active and passive labour market measures is not uncontested. To begin with,

Table 3.1: Active labour market and unemployment benefit spending, 2003			
	Active labour market policy (ALMP) spending (% of GDP)	Unemployment benefit spending (% of GDP)	ALMP spending as % of unemployment benefit spending
Australia	0.4	0.7	57.1
Denmark	1.5	3.3	45.5
France	1.3	1.9	68.4
Germany	1.1	1.8	61.1
Iceland	0.1	0.5	20.0
Netherlands	1.5	1.6	93.8
New Zealand	0.5	0.8	62.5
Norway	0.8	0.7	114.3
United States	0.2	0.5	40.0

Source: OECD (2007a)

its focus on *public* employment services – that is, those operated by the state – disregards private sector activity. In some countries, privately operated recruitment agencies actually play a larger role than those operated by the state. Similarly, private businesses operate forms of job training and apprenticeships that are important in many countries but are not taken account of in the above OECD figures.

More importantly, however, activation of unemployed people or income protection against the contingency of joblessness is only part of the many ways in which states can and do influence the functioning of national economies and labour markets. It is common sense that unemployment is dependent on the overall economic situation. As a consequence, sound economic policies that promote economic growth and stability are often seen as the most effective employment policies. Interestingly, while empirical research seems to verify the negative link between unemployment and economic performance, the fundamental question about how best to encourage growth is a far from technical one. All around the world, policy makers, professionals and academics still engage in heated political debates on this important issue (see Box 3.1).

In addition, several other dimensions of social policy also have an influence on employment levels. In particular, *education* and *immigration policies* have to be mentioned at this point as they not only influence the number of people seeking employment but also the skills base of national labour forces (see also Chapter Four). *Family policies* often determine how much parents struggle to reconcile working careers and family life as the provision of childcare in particular has a positive effect on overall employment rates. *Labour market regulations* such as mechanisms of wage setting and rules relating to employment contracts – determining, for instance, the number of working hours, holidays or the membership and density of union membership and work councils across industries – also have an impact on both employers' and employees' work and employment decisions.

A thorough account of employment policies cannot be content with differentiating merely between passive and active policy measures alone, but must take note of all of the above mechanisms.

Box 3.1	Unemployment – which unemployment?

According to the standard definition by the International Labour Organization (ILO), the term **unemployment** refers to people who are without work, are available for work and are actively seeking work (www.ilo.org). The **unemployment rate**, which is most commonly reported in the media coverage around the globe, refers to the share of unemployed people of the so-called **labour force**. This labour force is itself calculated as the sum of all people employed and unemployed.

It is important to understand that unemployment rates do not refer to levels of **economic inactivity**. The reasons why unemployed people in the prime labour market age range (25-64 years) are not available for or are actively seeking work are manifold: parents may decide to disrupt their working career during child rearing; others may take time off to care for their frail parents or other family members; workers who look back at long working careers may opt to retire prior to the legal pension age if the corresponding rules allow them to do so. **Inactivity rates** thus measure the proportion of people of working age who are not in the labour force – that is, who are neither employed nor unemployed. The level of inactivity is usually noticeably higher than the level of unemployment. Many argue that the former is a much better indicator for the success of 'activation policies'.

While international organisations like the ILO or the OECD have made great progress in standardising unemployment and inactivity rates, many countries still use registered unemployed figures for official statements – they simply count how many unemployed people claim unemployment-related benefit at any given time. While such data are much easier to obtain than self-reported unemployment based on large-scale household panel surveys (this is the preferred data by the ILO and OECD), it is severely flawed as it excludes all those unemployed people who are not entitled to, or choose not to claim, such benefits. Thus, registered unemployment figures do not contain those unemployed people receiving income support or other forms of social assistance. As barriers to claiming unemployment-related benefits vary substantially across different nations (see Chapter Two), registered unemployment figures are not comparable.

Full employment has been the manifested goal of many governments around the world. However, it has been stressed that full employment should not be understood as a situation in which the unemployment rate is 0%. Instead, people who are simply between two different jobs are called **frictionally unemployed**. For example, if a constructer's contracted work has finished, it may take some time for him to find another assignment. It is widely accepted that this form of unemployment is not very problematic and will always persist even in nations with extraordinarily strong economies.

Structural unemployment is caused by fundamental change in the demand for certain workers and skills. These can become obsolete if economies change their operations. For example, the use of more efficient machinery has been one of the main causes of both productivity growth and elimination of labour in the agriculture and manufacturing sectors. In a globalised world, competitor nations might simply be able to produce certain goods at lower prices, thus resulting in the relocation of economic activity to these countries; for example, large parts of textile industries have been moved out of the relatively 'expensive' high-income countries since the mid-1970s. The mass-scale introduction of computers – combined with a series of mergers of transnational corporations in order to reduce administrative costs – has led to lay-offs of thousands of employees in banking and other service sectors across the world. Attempts to contain government budgets in order to keep taxation low have also led to substantial reductions of the number of public employees in many countries.

Structural changes of the economy are among the main reasons for prolonged spells of unemployment today. Definitions for long-term unemployment differ, but typically they refer to unemployment spells longer than 12 or even 24 months. The real danger for workers is not having to find identical work for another employer after a brief spell of unemployment (as in the case of frictional unemployment); the real danger is to lose employment in a particular branch of the economy and to be forced to find employment in a branch that requires very different skills. It is these forced career changes that are most regularly associated with long-term unemployment, which – in turn – poses a real poverty risk. Not least, long-term unemployment puts the most considerable strain on social security budgets as long-term unemployed people are the prime recipients of most of the different demand- and supply-side policy measures discussed in this chapter.

Key policy goals

Unemployment is among the main causes of poverty, social exclusion and social inequality. It is often related to serious personal and social problems such as stress, low self-esteem, marital breakdown and ill-health. The seriousness of unemployment increases with its duration, while the length of unemployment spells itself is among the most important determinants of an individual's employment prospects. The 'employability' of excluded individuals from the labour market decreases substantially with time.

For governments, unemployment tends to inflate budget deficits as spending for passive and active unemployment measures rise automatically with the number of recipients. At the same time, increases in unemployment can lead to reductions in tax revenues as jobless people are often exempt from paying income tax, national insurance contributions and sometimes even VAT. As a consequence, governments may be forced to increase taxes and contributions for the working population or to cut government spending for education, healthcare or the infrastructure.

The aim of boosting labour market participation rates – that is, the aim of getting as many people into paid employment as possible – has been at the heart of attempts to alleviate social disadvantages and to promote social inclusion. Added to this, demographic changes in many countries mean that **dependency ratios** (the ratio of children and pensioners to people of working age) are projected to grow substantially in the course of the next 20 to 30 years, making the increase of employment rates a necessity if existing welfare state arrangements are to be financed without very significant tax rises.

In recent years, traditional social security or income protection schemes have increasingly been under attack for being detrimental to the goal of boosting labour market participation rates. It has been argued that what we have called passive benefits effectively reduce labour supply which in turn leads to slower economic growth, higher structural unemployment and eventually further strains on state budgets. For example, it is claimed that unemployed individuals who receive too generous unemployment benefits have an incentive to delay their return to work. Rather than encouraging jobless people to seek paid employment, passive social security or income protection is seen as the cause of a **dependency culture**. Terms like unemployment or poverty traps are often mentioned in connection with these arguments. Consequently, activation has been promoted as the single dominant goal of employment policies by policy makers in many different countries.

In reality, employment rates differ quite substantially from country to country. Data on labour market participation is not available for all countries around the world, but ILO estimates suggest that the share of employed and self-employed people as a proportion of the total working-age population does not usually exceed the 80% mark. Most of the countries in Figure 3.1 reached employment rates of between 60% and just over 70%. There are, however, some countries with rates of only around or even well below 50%. This tells us that despite the aim to bring as many people as possible into paid employment there is still significant room for improvement in most countries.

We should not, however, overemphasise the issue of the quantity of work in promoting well-being, for the *quality* of work is equally important here. High levels of employment and economic progress are not sufficient if workers are restricted from sharing the wealth that they helped to create. For example, the ILO has fought to make freedom of association

Figure 3.1: Employment rates

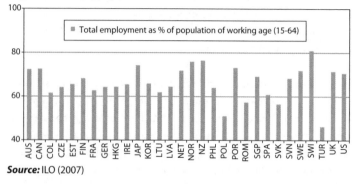

Source: ILO (2007)

(that is, the right to join a trade union), elimination of compulsory and child labour as well as the elimination of gender, religious and racial discrimination at the workplace a reality. To date, 178 countries have committed themselves to the different ILO conventions. While the ILO has achieved its goal for many workers, it is still a long way short of doing so for all workers across the world.

Inside the EU, the European Social Chapter requires member states to adopt policies to guarantee non-discriminatory remuneration, a minimum working age of 16 years, maximum hours of work per week, minimum health and social security provision (including minimum pension rights) and free association in trades unions and collective bargaining (find more information at: http://europa.eu). The proposal of the Social Chapter triggered serious disputes among the EU member countries at first and only with some delay did all EU member states agree to sign it eventually. These provisions go beyond those in the ILO conventions, highlighting key issues about workplace safety and even remuneration that fall under the umbrella of employment policy. In some countries the state plays a significant role in regulating labour market pay in an effort to ensure that work delivers a living wage. Some also regulate contracts to guard against the easy dismissal of employees in order to promote greater stability of employment.

These examples illustrate that there are significant variations across countries in terms of the specific tools used to expand labour market participation and in terms of what is understood as the most favourable level of labour market protection for employees. The illustration of different replacement rates for long-term unemployed people in Chapter Two gave a first indication of this. We will now expand on this in more detail.

Key delivery mechanisms

The ways in which countries try to maintain high levels of employment are manifold. To make some sense of the various policy tools at the disposal of state governments, the literature broadly separates out between so-called **demand-** and **supply-side** policy instruments that can be used to influence national labour markets. Unemployment occurs – according to this view – if there is an imbalance between the supply of labour (that is, the number of people seeking work) and the demand for labour (that is, the number of jobs on offer from employers). Supply-side policies aim to increase the number of people (or, more specifically, the number of people with the necessary skills) looking for work, while demand-side policies aim to create the economic conditions that will lead employers to need more workers.

Communist-style socialist economic planning has offered the most direct and radical approach to managing the demand side of the labour market. For instance, at the height of its socialist planning system, all jobs in China were allocated by the government's labour bureaux. Jobs were guaranteed for life and wages determined by the state. Since the late 1970s, the Chinese system has been significantly reformed, but the state (not least through state-owned enterprises) is still at the heart of the economy. Although this is an extreme example, it is worth noting that, historically at least, capitalist economies have also engaged heavily in direct job creation as a means of sustaining high employment levels. Indeed, a central plank of so-called **Keynesian economics** was the notion that states could smooth out peaks and troughs in demand by injecting public money into the economy when unemployment was rising. In many countries, the post-war years saw an expansion of state ownership in the economy as a consequence; in the UK, for instance, the state once owned and controlled many key businesses in the fields of transport, motor vehicle production, telecommunications and energy production. Employees in these state-owned industries were, to a degree, insulated from downward swings in the economy because the state could use public money to cover shortfalls in income and so avoid the need for job losses. Indeed, many of these industries were in fact initially nationalised (that is, moved from private hands into state ownership) in order to protect against job losses that would have otherwise occurred.

While programmes of nationalisation have lost some of their attractiveness since the 1980s – many economists argued that they led to the state subsidising inefficient businesses or unpopular products and many nationalisations were reversed through programmes of privatisation as a consequence – examples of Keynesian-type labour market programmes can still be found, although the investment tends to be in areas of the economy that are less likely to be seen as part of the private sector's domain. A good example of such an initiative is South Africa's Expanded Public Works Programme (EPWP), which was formally announced in 2003 (www.epwp.gov.za/). This government initiative aimed to create up to 750,000 jobs by investing in the construction and improvement of existing roads, water drains and urban sidewalks between 2004 and 2009. It aimed to create a further 300,000 jobs through various environmental projects as well as in the social and cultural sectors in South Africa. The EPWP has played a crucial role in the South African government's attempt to tackle unemployment and its overall goal of creating more than one million jobs is clearly of huge importance. This public works programme echoes one of the most famous early attempts to use the state's spending power to combat unemployment: the US's New Deal programme that was implemented as a response to the Great Depression of the 1930s.

It should also be noted that most countries directly employ considerable numbers of people in public services such as health and education that are at the core of the welfare state and as members of the civil service, judicial system and police and armed forces. Through its control of these services the state is more often than not the biggest single employer in a country and any attempt to expand or contract public services can have an important impact on employment levels. Indeed, in the 1980s and early 1990s, Sweden used the expansion of its welfare services as both a tool for guarding against rising unemployment during a major recession of the world economy and as a strategy for increasing the participation rate of women in the labour market. Contrarily, the introduction of arguably more efficient and cost-effective new public management methods in Germany led to many public sector workers being made redundant during the 1990s and early 2000s. While this was dubbed as a necessary step to modernise public services in Germany, it undoubtedly aggravated the already tense situation in the German labour market during those years.

Finally, governments often aim to influence demand via **fiscal policy**. While large-scale nationalisation of businesses is off the cards politically in many nations, some governments still resort to Keynesian-inspired demand management ideas by looking to reduce taxation during times of low demand. Crudely put, the aim here is to inject extra money into the economy via tax cuts in the hope that people will spend this money and so, in turn, help reinvigorate the economy. The downside of cutting taxation is that governments have to then borrow money to cover the spending that taxes would have covered. In classic Keynesian thought, these **budget deficits** would need to be recovered by increased taxes once the economy was in better health.

As hinted above, there has been a significant shift in thinking in recent years that has taken governments away from demand management techniques. Instead, employment policies have increasingly focused on supply-side measures and, in particular, active labour market policies (ALMPs). This shift has not been without its critics, many of whom have seen it as a process of weakening citizens' social rights and increasing their obligations.

It is not hard to see why some people have made this case. Historically, the first forms of social insurance in the pioneer welfare states granted compensation for workers and their families in cases of occupational disease and work injury, thus indicating a sense of responsibility on the states' or employers' side in cases in which workers lose the ability to gain a labour market income through no fault of their own. The subsequent – and often quite significantly delayed – implementation of unemployment benefit systems has to be seen in the light of a growing understanding of the existence of **economic cycles** and the notion that markets may simply not create enough of the demanded employment at times. The relative generosity of unemployment benefits in countries such as Sweden has thus been sometimes explained as a kind of state insurance against the insecurity of world markets.

Much of the thrust of the activation agenda goes against this grain because it attempts to make the payment of unemployment benefits *conditional* on citizens' participation in schemes that will make them more employable. For instance, in many countries receipt of benefit is only available to long-term unemployed people if they agree to participate in labour market training or subsidised employment. In some countries, citizens may have their benefit withdrawn if they refuse to accept a job that the state deems suitable even if the citizen is qualified to work in quite a different field.

Thereby, the increased conditionality of benefits can be seen as part of a broader set of strategies that aim to **make work pay** by reducing the overall generosity of support for unemployed people and in many countries the unemployment benefit payment levels have also been reduced as part of this process. Rather than stressing the cyclical nature of the economy and the need for social protection against economic downturns, the thrust of these reforms has been to stress the responsibility of individuals to find work and – as already mentioned above – the risks of generous benefits reducing incentives for individuals to find work.

Another set of supply-side policies that have become popular with governments in recent years have focused around attempts to increase the flexibility of rigid labour markets. The question of employment protection is an important one. Similar to the critique of passive social security measures, rigid labour markets have been attacked for creating barriers for employment as they are said to limit the speed with which businesses can respond to short-term increases or decreases of work orders, for example.

Yet the stringent regulation of hiring and firing is but one feature of a rigid labour market. In some countries, employers' associations have argued that permissible hours of work are too tightly regulated and compensation for overtime work too generous to enable businesses to adjust their production to short-term changes in demand for goods. It has also been argued that powerful trades unions can prevent flexibility by protecting incumbent workers to the detriment of labour market outsiders more generally. Others have stressed that the costs of employers contributing to the healthcare and pensions costs of their employees can act as a disincentive to them employing extra workers, particularly if the global market allows them to shift production to countries where there are fewer requirements to make such contributions. As a consequence of all this, some countries have looked to water down employment protections in the belief that a less rigid labour market will remove barriers to employment growth by attracting international investments.

However, it would be wrong to suggest that supply-side activation strategies are all about increasing obligations and reducing rights. In reality, ALMPs typically feature a mix of carrots and sticks (see Box 3.2 on the South Korean case). For example, make work pay strategies are not exclusively about increasing the conditionality of unemployment benefits. Many governments have also tried to encourage employment of long-term unemployed people by reducing employers' costs of hiring people in the low-wage labour sector. Governments can do this by either granting subsidies to employers to hire long-term unemployed people or by decreasing non-wage labour costs (for example, by shifting the financing of income protection systems away from employers' social contributions to general taxation). Many countries have introduced programmes that help unemployed people set up small businesses – that is, to encourage the transition from unemployment into self-employment. In addition, many governments have increased the use of **in-work benefits** by, for example, topping up low-wage workers' income through **tax credits** in an attempt to remove the poverty traps that many benefit claimants face (see Chapter Two). On a similar note, **national minimum wage** schemes are designed to raise the disposable incomes of workers with low earnings.

Improved family policies have also been identified as a crucial strategy for increasing employment rates as they make it easier for parents – particularly women – to reconcile family life and working careers. Empirical evidence suggests a clear link between policy measures such as free basic education for children, the existence of all-day schools, generous maternity leave schemes and good childcare on the one hand and the number of women joining the labour force on the other. Some nations have therefore looked to considerably strengthen policies in these areas as part of their efforts to boost employment rates.

Box 3.2   ALMPs in South Korea

During the 1980s and early 1990s, South Korea was famous –
along with Hong Kong, Singapore and Taiwan – as one of the so-
called 'tiger economies'. Rapid industrialisation saw South Korea
play an increasingly important role in the global manufacturing
economy and this, in turn, delivered rapid economic growth,
increasing national wealth and strong levels of employment.

In 1997, however, South Korea was hit very badly by a relatively
sudden economic crash that affected much of East Asia.
Unemployment began to rise quite rapidly and a new mood
of economic uncertainty swept over the country. Income
protection schemes were relatively immature at the time and
rising poverty levels in the wake of the crash highlighted the
inadequacy of many social security policies. At the same time,
however, the crash also highlighted some structural weaknesses
in the South Korean economy, not least in its labour market.

South Korea responded by trying to improve both the strength
of income protection schemes and the flexibility of its labour
markets at the same time. They dubbed the strategy 'productive
welfarism' on the basis that it aimed to protect the well-being
of citizens in times of need while also producing higher levels
of economic productivity. One side of the equation entailed
expanding the coverage of the unemployment insurance
scheme and introducing a nationwide social assistance safety
net; the other side of the equation involved spending more on
ALMPs in order to help unemployed people find work while also
removing labour market protections in order to make it easier
for employers to sack employees.

The ALMPs introduced or expanded in the wake of the economic
crisis had many components. These included an expansion of
training programmes for those registering for unemployment
benefits; indeed, around 20% of unemployed people attended

such courses in the years following the crash. In addition, there was an expansion of employment protection programmes that subsidised the wages of workers in firms that would otherwise have sacked workers and employment promotion programmes that subsidised the wages of key groups of disadvantaged unemployed workers that firms might not have otherwise recruited. Benefit claimants can sometimes receive bonus payments if they find work especially quickly.

The South Korean system has strict job-search rules for those who claim benefits when out of work. For instance: it is necessary to register with the national employment agency at the same time as applying for benefit; when receiving benefits, claimants are required to regularly demonstrate that they are looking for jobs and will have their benefits stopped if they cannot do so; and benefit payment is suspended if the claimant rejects a job recommended by the national employment agency.

While some are sceptical about the merits of the approach – and the OECD has suggested that more needs to be done in terms of strengthening some employment rights and targeting ALMPs towards those who need most help – the South Korean government claims that productive welfarism has given equal weight to both social and economic policy objectives and points to its success since the crash in delivering growth in social spending while also improving economic performance.

Key policy issues

What are, perhaps, the core dilemmas in employment policy are no doubt implicit in the above discussion: there is often a tension (or a perceived tension) between measures designed to promote the quantity of jobs and those designed to improve the quality of jobs. And, similarly, there is a tension between efforts to protect citizens against the risks of unemployment and the risk that those protections may harm efforts to promote re-employment.

Indeed, the main rationale behind the growing emphasis on activation policies in many countries is that generous social security benefits reduce the supply of labour, which is at odds with the principal goal of employment policies to maintain and increase high levels of employment. Similar to the notion of the so-called **poverty traps** (see Chapter Two), some analysts have argued that income protection schemes can produce **unemployment traps**, which foster a culture of **welfare dependency**. Let us return to our example of differences in benefit generosity for long-term unemployed people introduced in Chapter Two: we might ask whether or not it is plausible to suggest that a long-term unemployed person in Sweden who receives 52% of their previous salary should be more inclined to remain out of paid employment for longer (for example, in order to wait for the 'right' job that fits their qualification and is close to their home) than a long-term unemployed person in the US who can only expect 7% of their previous income. Is it not evident, that an unemployed person receiving 52% of their previous salary should be much better able to maintain their living standard, while an unemployed person with 7% of their previous income will feel much more pressure in that sense?

Certainly, many policy makers seem to think that there are good reasons for making such claims, but the evidence is far from clear cut. The comparison of net unemployment benefit replacement rates (a commonly used indicator to measure the generosity of unemployment benefit systems) with incidences of long-term unemployment caution us against jumping to rash conclusions (see Figure 3.2). Several countries in the OECD with the highest net unemployment replacement rates (for example, Denmark, the Netherlands and Sweden) do not suffer from excessive long-term unemployment in relative terms. Similarly, some countries with the highest share of long-term unemployed people among the jobless only show average or even very low net unemployment replacement rates (see, for example, Greece). Long-term unemployment has been a serious issue in Italy although this country has the least generous unemployment benefit system among the countries presented in Figure 3.2; Norway – the country with the lowest rate of long-term unemployment in the OECD (apart from South Korea) – is commonly seen as having one of the most generous social security

Figure 3.2: Net replacement rates and long-term unemployment, 2002/03

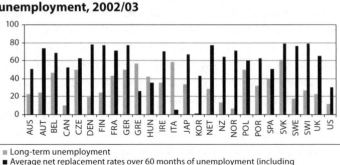

■ Long-term unemployment
■ Average net replacement rates over 60 months of unemployment (including social assistance)

Notes: People unemployed for 12 months or more as a percentage of total unemployed; average percentage of the net income that unemployment benefit replaces (including social assistance) for two earnings levels and four family situations.

Source: OECD (2006b)

systems worldwide. Unfortunately, similar data are still hard to come by for countries outside the OECD, but we have no reason to believe that such an automatism between unemployment benefit generosity and long-term unemployment actually exists in the middle- and low-income countries.

At the same time, it would be wrong to suggest that unemployment traps are not a real issue in many countries. The fact that disposable income can potentially drop with acceptance of employment in the low-income sector is a reality for many unemployed people. Moreover, there is some evidence suggesting that placement efforts, increased obligations and conditionality can help to bring unemployed people back into work faster. The statistics presented in Figure 3.2 merely intend to suggest that while supply-side activation policies undoubtedly have some positive effects, they should not be seen as a panacea to the problems in contemporary labour markets.

Indeed, one major limitation of active labour market programmes is that they only work if the increased supply of labour they create matches demand in the labour market. Supply-side activation policies do not create jobs by themselves. A particular issue here is that structural changes in national economies often lead to the dismissal of workers whose specific skills have lost their value in the labour market. This has happened in many high-income countries as a by-product of the transformation from manufacturing-based industrial economies towards service-based, knowledge economies. Processes of **deindustrialisation** pose real challenges for employment policy. The closure of an industry that provided employment for a large number of workers in a area can be devastating for a whole city or region and activation policies can do little when there are thousands of workers with unwanted skills all looking for re-employment in the same place at the same time. For such workers – many of whom might well be in their forties or fifties and look back at long working careers – cutbacks of benefits and increased conditionality will have an uncertain impact on their employment prospects but will almost certainly increase their risk of falling into poverty.

Mismatches in the skills level of national labour forces and the demand in national economies have increasingly become a reality in many countries. Thus, policy makers are facing the paradox that long-term unemployment often persists at relatively high levels, while employers complain that they cannot find sufficiently skilled personnel to staff job vacancies. One possible route for governments out of this dilemma has been to increase efforts to attract highly skilled workers from foreign countries – a strategy that has, unfortunately, often been instrumentalised by populist parties. Skills shortages are also becoming a more and more important issue in emerging economies around the world. The pattern is very similar: although countries like China and India have comparably large labour forces at their disposal, foreign companies have warned that they often cannot find Chinese or Indian nationals with skills and qualifications that are in demand. Hence, developing more comprehensive education systems has become a top priority in these countries (see also Chapter Four).

Despite the problems of deindustrialisation that most high-income countries have faced, their overall employment rates have generally witnessed an upward trend. Increases in female labour market participation have been formidable since the 1960s in particular. However, many of the newly created jobs in these countries are less secure than the ones they have replaced: many are temporary, part time or jobholders are subject to slimmer chances of being promoted over the years. While this is not necessarily a negative development – job-splitting and work-sharing initiatives have gained attention in recent years – it has been suggested that a shift towards a more knowledge-based economy has produced a growing divide between those with high skills who are more likely to be in well-paid and secure jobs and those with low skills who are more likely to be in low-paid and insecure jobs. Certainly it is the case that income inequality has increased in many countries as the labour market has changed and that the only chance for many long-term unemployed and low-skilled youths to find employment is often in the low-income sector. It is also the case that in the emerging knowledge economies the risk of becoming unemployed – and of remaining in unemployment for a long period – is strongly associated with educational and professional qualifications.

It is partly because of this that many states have begun to stress the importance of *investment in human capital* (that is, the education and training of individuals) as both an economic and social strategy: in other words, equitable access to quality education and training from an early age is key for future working careers. Indeed, more and more policy makers suggest that this is a route to squaring the often competing objectives of social and economic policy, although such arguments have fierce critics.

One of the main criticisms of this thinking is that it may do more to help those with strong skills and high levels of education than it helps those without. Indeed, people who work in the growing low-income sector can often find that their wages alone are not sufficient to lift them out of poverty; this is particularly so if – as is happening in some countries – the financial rewards going to those in high-skill occupations are increasing at a much faster rate than the rewards for those in lower-skill occupations. In fact, some countries have experienced a growing number of **working poor**.

While the introduction of a minimum wage is seen as an important tool to help alleviate this problem, the question of what level of income is perceived as a sufficient minimum is important here. About three quarters of EU member states had some form of statutory national minimum wage in 2006 (see Table 3.2), but the rates varied from merely €0.62 in Romania to €8.27 in France. To some extent these differences reflect variations in the costs of living in those countries, but the setting of minimum wages is always a political question too.

Table 3.2: National minimum wages (adult rate, €, gross), 2006	
Country	**Hourly rate**
Czech Republic	1.70
Estonia	1.14
France	8.27
Hungary	1.36
Ireland	7.65
Latvia	0.88
Lithuania	1.06
Romania	0.62
Slovakia	1.17
United Kingdom	7.85
Source: European Industrial Relations Observatory (2007)	

Indeed, critics argue that minimum wages can actually increase poverty if they prevent jobs being created or lead to employers laying off workers because increased wage costs would render jobs no longer profitable. It is because of such fears that arguments to increase the level of the minimum wage (or to introduce one altogether) often face such opposition. As an alternative, in some countries, such as the UK and US, the minimum wage remains modest, but tax credits are used instead to top up the wages of some low-income households. However, in-work benefits suffer from the same problems as the means-tested benefits discussed in Chapter Two.

Another issue for countries implementing ALMPs is the *sustainability of employment*. Many countries have put mechanisms in place to ensure that job placement is not only short term, as high return rates of unemployed people to ALMPs of different sorts would certainly not be a positive policy outcome. One could also argue that it is not enough to simply place the most vulnerable in society into employment without offering some form of additional mentoring to ensure that they can cope with their new life situations. On a similar note, state subsidies to encourage employment of long-term unemployed people, to protect national companies (or sectors) from international competition or to save businesses from bankruptcy are often popular among the electorate, but opponents of such initiatives have argued that they are not always beneficial in the long run as they can be detrimental to the prospects of other companies in the same industrial branch and so weaken the economy overall. In addition, evaluations of state subsidies for employers have shown that they have not always been very successful in helping the jobless into permanent employment.

Of course, as noted above, the state itself is a major employer and temporary employment programmes in the public sector such as public works schemes can be used to help unemployed citizens sharpen their skills or demonstrate to potential employers their readiness for work. More concretely, the state can also choose to expand employment in the public services. This has the advantage of creating secure, well-paid and skilled jobs. However, the public sector in general has been attacked in recent years and most governments have been under pressure to reduce public sector employment. Indeed, one of the areas of work that some countries have transferred into the private sector has been the delivery of services to help unemployed people back into work (see Box 3.3).

Box 3.3   Public or private? Employment services in the Netherlands

The majority of this chapter has focused on the ways in which the state can use its power to boost both the quantity and the quality of jobs. However, we should not overlook the clear fact that the private sector, ultimately, makes many of the key decisions that determine the overall levels of employment in society. In practice, the activities of the state interlink with the activities of private businesses in this field of policy and there are some difficult questions about where the boundaries of public – as opposed to private – activities should lie. As noted, in its attempts to guard employment the state can subsidise businesses or even nationalise them, but in so doing can have a negative impact on other competing or related businesses.

Recent years have witnessed a rolling back of the state's role in some areas of employment policy, but one particularly interesting – and, perhaps, unusual – development has been the privatisation of employment services themselves in some countries. In the Netherlands, for instance, recent reforms have seen the services for those who are hardest to place in employment transferred from the state-managed Centres for Work and Income to a series of private organisations. These private companies receive payment from the state partly on the basis of the number of clients referred to them, partly on the basis of the sorts of services they provide and partly on the basis of whether or not the client is successfully placed into employment. The services they offer cover the same kinds of activities provided by state employment agencies such as training, job-search advice and post-employment mentoring, but one of the aims of the policy is to encourage a diversity of competing providers able to offer a more diverse and flexible range of programmes that reflect the diverse needs of the jobseekers.

Evidence regarding the impact of the reforms has so far been mixed – in part because contracts have proved too complex and activities difficult to monitor – but the private provision of (public) employment services is now a clear feature of the Dutch system.

This brings us to the last and maybe most important point of the discussion. Some have argued that generous forms of social security, strong labour market regulations and high public spending are no longer sustainable in times of **globalisation**. In order to remain attractive for foreign investment and to achieve necessary productivity gains in the future – so goes the argument – social security has to become leaner and labour markets more flexible. Across the high-income countries of the OECD, employment policy becoming 'lean' and 'flexible' means many being deprived of social rights that were offered to past generations. There are many reasons to suggest that this is part of a necessary modernisation process in order to maintain the levels of wealth and overall employment in these countries. We have addressed what lies behind these arguments in the previous sections of this chapter. We have also shown that employment policy in the broad sense plays a major role in promoting both economic prosperity and social well-being.

Yet the complexity and interaction of different policy mechanisms makes it very difficult indeed to evaluate and separate the outcomes of single measures; indeed we are only beginning to really understand many of the long-term effects of certain macroeconomic and social policies. The empirical evidence for many of the crucial policy dilemmas raised in this section is still inconclusive. Answers to whether one or another employment policy is preferable are often 'political', as are answers to whether a 'lean' or a 'generous' welfare state is more conducive to economic growth and the creation of jobs. While globalisation has undoubtedly changed the conditions under which national employment policies have to function today, answers as to how to react to these changes are still disputed. It is likely that trades unions' and employers' representatives have a very different idea about the policy solutions indeed.

SUMMARY

■ Employment policy is often reduced to a distinction between **passive** and **active labour market programmes**; however, this is a simplification of a much broader field of policy.

■ The main goal of employment policy is to reach and maintain **high employment rates** under acceptable working conditions.

■ Employment policy can be divided into **supply-** and **demand-side measures**, but the emphasis in recent years has been on the former.

■ Long-term unemployment is still among the most significant factors causing **poverty**; but job placement alone does not always end this condition.

■ **Globalisation** has triggered a hard-fought debate about competitiveness and social security; while the empirical evidence is somewhat inconclusive, the preference of the two is still – primarily – a political decision.

READING GUIDE

Mooney (2004) provides a good overview of the complex interactions between work and social policy more generally. Van Berkel and Møller (2002) offer a useful analysis of the 'active social policy' agenda in Europe. Lødemel and Trickey (2001) present detailed case studies of workfare programmes in several high-income countries. Goul Andersen and Jensen (2002) offer a broad overview of changing employment and unemployment policies across Europe, while Carpenter et al (2007) examine the bigger picture of how work has become centrally embedded in welfare to such an extent that some view the term 'workfare state' more appropriate than 'welfare state'. Hayward and James (2004) explore issues surrounding skills and employment.

Internet resources on macroeconomic development around the world are many and relatively easy to find. Readers interested in statistics on GDP growth, inflation rates, unemployment as well as structural changes of labour markets will find a library of statistical information on the web:

the ILO's labour statistics (LABORSTA) has probably been the primary source of such information (http://laborsta.ilo.org/). The International Monetary Fund's (IMF's) World Economic Outlook (www.imf.org/) and the OECD's Annual Labour Force Statistics and Employment Outlook all provide similar statistics (www.oecd.org). On a smaller scale geographically, statistics are also provided by the Statistical Bureau of the European Union (Eurostat) (http://epp.eurostat.ec.europa.eu/) and the Asian Development Bank (www.adb.org).

Apart from providing numerical information, the ILO has also been concerned with monitoring and bettering the conditions of workers around the world – its webpage – www.ilo.org – contains a list of valuable publications for students interested in the link between employment and social protection. Similarly, the OECD provides timely discussions, research reports and news articles on contemporary employment issues on its webpage (www.oecd.org).

4

education

Introduction

Access to education is a fundamental human right. Article 26 of the *Universal Declaration of Human Rights* (UN General Assembly, 1948) stresses that every child should have access to free elementary education. In addition, it states that professional education should be made 'generally available' and that access to higher education should be 'determined by merit only' and thus not be subject to racial, gender, religious or any other form of discrimination. The Article continues by emphasising that education ought to be 'directed to the full development of the human personality', 'strengthening of respect for human rights', the 'promotion of understanding, tolerance and friendship' and eventually 'the maintenance of peace'.

In reality, education policy is developed with both *social* (even *cultural*) and *economic* goals in mind. Indeed, it has been suggested that the economic significance of education is greater than ever because of a global transition towards **knowledge-based societies** in which intellectual innovation becomes the primary means to secure economic growth. In recent years, education policy has increasingly been at the centre of debates regarding the competitiveness of national economies, labour market participation, social inclusion and social cohesion. In this sense education policy is very similar to the pillars discussed in Chapter One.

Because of this diversity of policy aims, and this too is similar to the previously discussed pillars of social policy, what exactly is meant by 'education policy' can be hard to pin down. Most typically, education policy has been conceptualised by means of a division into three main levels or stages of education: from the fundamental stages in the **pre-primary and primary** education sector that caters for the youngest children; to **secondary** education that provides the main focus of formal schooling, not least in terms of the formal qualifications school leavers are expected to gain; and finally **tertiary** education that caters for those who study beyond the school level by, for instance, undertaking university-level qualifications. The actual ages at which students typically pass from primary to secondary to tertiary education can vary considerably across countries and there are major differences between countries in terms of how education services are structured at each of these levels.

The scale and importance of education policies can be crudely indicated by the large amounts of public money most governments allocate to this field of activity (see Table 4.1). In high-income countries, an average of around 6.5% of GDP is devoted to education spending by governments, although the actual figures range from below 5% in places like Germany to in excess of 8% in some of the Scandinavian countries. Upper middle-income countries display similar patterns, but with a slightly lower average spend. In the low- and lower middle-income countries, however, much more variation in spending is evident, with some – such as the Maldives and Lesotho – devoting very large amounts of national income to education, while others – such as Bangladesh and El Salvador – allocating rather modest proportions of GDP.

In most countries the state is the main provider of education. However, a **mixed economy of provision** is the reality in most places, with public provision being supplemented by private activity. As we will see later in this chapter, the public–private mix in education shows some important variation across the globe, for while many of the highest-spending nations – particularly in Scandinavia – source almost all of the education spending from public funds, there are other countries – the US, South Korea and Chile, for example – in which substantial private spending plays a hugely significant role alongside public spending.

While education is usually thought of in terms of the activity that takes places in schools, colleges and universities, a broader definition might also

Table 4.1: Education expenditure (public spending as % of GDP), 2002-05

High-income countries	
Denmark	8.5
United States	5.9
Netherlands	5.4
Germany	4.6
Upper middle-income countries	
Costa Rica	4.9
Mauritius	4.5
Russian Federation	3.6
Lower middle-income countries	
Lesotho	13.4
Maldives	7.1
Iran (Islamic Republic of)	4.7
El Salvador	2.8
Low-income countries	
Malawi	5.8
Senegal	5.4
Bangladesh	2.5

Sources: UNDP (2007) and World Bank (2007) country classifications

encompass various forms of (on-the-job) vocational training (see Box 4.1) and (non-vocational) 'lifelong' adult learning. Future-oriented research and development activities conducted by research centres belonging to private companies or state agencies may also have real significance for the education and skills development of nations. If 'human development' is one of the core goals of education, one may even ask whether public libraries, museums and other cultural institutions (operas, theatre) fall under the realm of education policy.

Box 4.1	Continuing vocational training in comparative perspective

In 2003, the European Commission published its final assessment of the Second European Continuing Vocational Training Survey (European Commission, 2002). This survey included around 76,000 businesses across the 25 EU member countries. It uncovered some striking differences in the provision of, and access to, continuing vocational training schemes across the EU.

Two forms of continuing vocational training are distinguished in the report: first, 'classical' forms of continuing vocational training, which include courses, workshops and seminars offered both within and outside of enterprises; and second, 'other' forms of continual vocational training, which include instructions by colleagues as well as job adjustment, rotation and exchange programmes.

Only about half of the businesses surveyed actually offered internal or external training courses to their employees. This average masks stark inequalities. The percentage of employers offering such courses was above 80% in Denmark, Sweden, the Netherlands and Norway compared to below 25% in most of the new Eastern European accession states as well as Portugal and Greece. The percentage of employees actually making use of these offers varied accordingly. While the merits of lifelong learning programmes have been highlighted by professionals, politicians and academics alike, the reality looks somewhat bleaker, with only about 50% of employees engaged in some form of classical continuing vocational training in the countries with the highest rates and, for the majority of countries, this rate was around or even well below 40%.

The argument that employers favour 'other' forms of continuing vocational training cannot be verified fully. According to the survey, just 37% of all employees benefited from on-the-job coaching and other job adjustment programmes. Only about 16% of all employers in the survey offered some kind of job rotation or exchange scheme to their workers. On the positive side, the latter forms of continuing vocational training have increased in almost all countries since the early 1990s.

It would be wrong, however, to point the finger just at the employers. In particular, there is some evidence to suggest that employees are hesitant to take part in job rotation and exchange programmes that are offered to them. All in all, it seems as if there is still room to improve the availability and access to continuing vocational training for many workers and employees and thus to make the ideal of an ever-improving skills base of the European workforce a reality.

Key policy goals

At the most basic level, education policy is designed to enable citizens to interact with society. In other words, education equips individuals to engage with their 'culture' – that is, the prevalent ideas, norms and beliefs in a given country. Thus, education is not only a tool to 'socialise' children and young people, but it also enables individuals to participate in societal or political processes. The historical development of education in European societies can be interpreted from this context. For instance, demands to make education available across all parts of society were closely linked with political struggles for greater democratisation (and vice versa) that took place in many European nations in the 19th century. In many nations, the expansion of democracy was accompanied by an expansion of education, not least because many governments recognised that if all citizens were to participate politically then they required an education in order to make informed choices. At the same time, by favouring or promoting a particular language or religion, the expansion of education also helped to create a common 'identity' and this was at the heart of nation-building processes in 18th- and 19th-century Europe. In short, from the earliest days of state expansion into the field of education, its role in promoting **social cohesion** has been recognised by policy makers.

Article 26 of the *Universal Declaration of Human Rights* (UN Assembly, 1948) aligns education policy closely with the issue of **human development**. From a global perspective, although not uncontested, the so-called UN Human Development Index has become one of the main tools to measure human development around the globe. Central to this index is the measurement of educational outcomes (particularly adult literacy and school enrolment) as the UN regard access to a decent education as an essential human right on the grounds that it plays a crucial role in allowing humans to develop and fulfil their potential. High human development countries typically have adult literacy rates above 90% and primary, secondary and tertiary education enrolment of above 80%. In low human development countries the respective figures plummet to around 50% and 40%. It is not unusual to find adult literacy and school enrolment rates between 25% and 35% in some of the lowest-income countries.

Education also has an important economic role. The term **human capital** is used as shorthand for the skills and qualifications possessed by individuals in the labour market. It has been used since the late 1950s, initially by economists who argue that – similar to investments in 'material capital' such as factories or machines – employers can achieve additional productivity gains by educating and training their workforce. For governments, increased education spending can be viewed as economic investment if it increases the level of human capital within the labour market. We should note that there is also an individual component here: an individual who enhances their own education and skills can often command a higher income in the labour market as a consequence.

Some have argued that education is becoming a more integral part of the economic and social strategy of national governments as a consequence of globalisation. The argument goes that high-income countries in particular must have extensive education policies in order to maintain their *competitive economic advantage in global markets* because they cannot compete with some of their low-wage competitors in terms of low manufacturing costs and taxation levels. Consequently, it is suggested, maintaining and enhancing the output of new industrial patents and other intellectual property is crucial to preserving levels of employment and affluence in these countries. To this end, delivering highly specialised, world-leading research via the education system can be an important part of a nation's economic innovation strategy.

However, we should also note that the prolongation of students' time spent in the education system – for instance by increasing the average minimum time to graduation in secondary and tertiary education or encouraging more people to attend university – has led to a reduction of labour supply in some countries. Employers' organisations often stress that skills and qualifications gained through education should correspond with those demanded in national economies. Indeed, the fact that some labour markets today are characterised by difficulties for employers in filling job vacancies while, at the same time, many people remain unemployed for long spells suggests that they might have a point. From an economic perspective, matching skills with labour market needs might also be an important goal of education policy and many governments try to influence the content of education curricula to this end. In particular, some nations stress the *vocational* dimensions of education much more strongly than others.

Education policy also has some much broader social aims. It is often argued that in a 'fair' society, the economic rewards that individuals reap (that is, income) ought, in some loose way, to be grounded in merit. For liberal theorists, this can only be so if there is a broad **equality of opportunity** in society. By giving all an 'equal start' in life, freely available universal education is seen by some as the guarantor of a broad equality of opportunity. Put bluntly, in an ideal world, it should be educational attainment (or 'merit') that determines a young person's future working career and not simply their family background.

However, such an argument only holds true if there is considerable **social mobility** in a nation. This term refers to individuals' ability to move across the hierarchical social class system of societies; the term depicts both upwards and downwards movement within an individual's own lifetime or from one generation to another. While the exact definition of 'social class' may vary in the literature, members of 'higher' classes are usually described by higher standards of living and professional qualifications (leading to more secure and more highly paid jobs). While it is generally accepted that education is a major factor in mediating social mobility, as we will see below many theorists point to broader obstacles to mobility that prevent more education from being a magic wand that can deliver equality of opportunity. Moreover, some even suggest that education itself can be such an obstacle, for if the education system favours the already well-off – for example, because access to the best schools or to universities is geared towards those from higher-income backgrounds – then qualifications may reinforce or even exacerbate divisions between social classes rather than ameliorate them. Consequently, some have argued that the 'equality of opportunity' perspective is flawed if there is not some evidence of a broader **equality of outcome** in terms of which groups of people are gaining educational awards and rewards.

All this points to the multifaceted and, in some cases, potentially conflicting goals of educational policy. Indeed, different nations place differing degrees of emphasis on these different goals. While, compared to social security (see Chapter Two), there is much less consensus among theorists in terms of what different 'types' of education system might look like in the higher-income countries, we can offer a broadly similar classification. For convenience, we will use the same labels that we used in Chapter Two.

First, there are **social democratic** types. In these countries, education is largely state funded and universally available and there is relatively strong social mobility. There is a strong concern with equality of outcome, with high education spending being matched by high social spending more generally. Sweden and Denmark are good examples.

Second, there are **liberal** types. Here the state devotes considerable levels of finance to education – albeit usually below levels in the social democratic types – but this is supplemented by considerable private expenditure so that, overall, a very high proportion of GDP is accounted for by education. In part because this private expenditure generally favours the better-off, but also because lower levels of social spending mean that social inequality also tends to be higher, there is less concern with equality of outcome in these nations and social mobility tends to be relatively low. The US is a good example.

Finally, there are **corporatist** types. Here the state tends to devote lower levels of national income to education than in the other two types, but relatively high social spending more generally means that inequality is not so high as in liberal types and social mobility is also greater. That said, there is typically a strong division between those undertaking academic and vocational education in these nations, with the latter being tied quite directly to labour market needs. Germany is a good example.

Hidden behind these cross-national differences are important differences in the key delivery mechanisms of education policy. It is these differences to which we now turn.

Key delivery mechanisms

Until recently 'education' has not featured as prominently as might be expected in the social policy literature. While the structure of this textbook has been inspired by Esping-Andersen's (1990) argument that we can find three different 'worlds of welfare', his seminal book did not mention 'education' at all. Similarly, while the OECD has collected a wide range of statistics on different education systems, these are presented separately from its data on social protection, the labour market and healthcare. Thus, statistics on social policy expenditure and financing collected by international organisations such as the OECD and ILO have not, rather bizarrely, accounted for 'education spending'.

As noted earlier, in most countries education consists of a mixed economy of public and private provision. In fact, as Figure 4.1 shows, the breakdown of public and private education funding varies somewhat from place to place. Some of the countries with highest overall levels of education spending rely almost completely on public sources of

Figure 4.1: Expenditure on educational institutions (as % of GDP), 2004

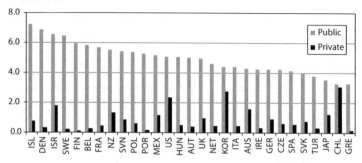

Notes: Public: includes public subsidies to households; also includes direct expenditure on educational institutions from international sources; private: net of public subsidies attributable for educational institutions.

Source: OECD (2007b)

funding (Denmark, Iceland, Finland and Sweden for instance). Yet, private education spending is very substantial in many other countries. In the cases of Chile, South Korea and the US, for instance, substantial private spending combines with public spending to bring the overall level of education spending close to or even beyond the spending levels in the above-mentioned Scandinavian countries. On average, the industrialised democracies of the OECD spent 5.7% of their respective GDP on education in the year 2004 and about 85% of these funds were for the public sector. The average for the non-OECD countries is generally slightly lower and smaller percentages of funding in these countries come from public bodies. This is indicative of the broader global picture, with private forms of education spending playing – on average – a bigger role in lower-income countries.

An analysis of public–private funding by different levels of education (that is, primary, secondary, tertiary) also shows much variation across nations. Generally, the role of private education is larger in tertiary education than in the other sectors. The cases of Chile and South Korea are interesting as tertiary education is almost entirely financed by private sources in these countries. In the US, there is a close to 2:1 split of public and private sources of finance for tertiary education spending. By contrast, in other countries – such as Belgium, Finland and Norway – 90% or more of tertiary-level spending comes from the public sector.

The complex interweaving of public and private service funding in most countries is usually matched by a similarly complex interweaving of public and private educational institutions. The most straightforward model comes in the form of state ownership of educational institutions such as schools and universities. In some countries the state is the dominant provider of education and so most educational institutions are publicly owned. However, such a model is far from being the norm. Indeed, privately owned for-profit and not-for-profit schools and colleges are widespread in many countries and in some this is the dominant form of provision. For instance, churches often run schools that provide a religious education alongside the standard curriculum taught in secular schools. In some countries ancient seats of learning that pre-date state intervention in education survive as private schools or colleges. While in some countries such private facilities can only be accessed by those with private funds (that is, those with sufficient cash to cover the tuition fees), in others the state allows the use of public funds to cover some or all of the costs of private education. In Austria, for instance, if private schools are established by officially recognised churches or religious bodies then the government covers the salary costs of all teachers in the school; all other private schools in Austria, however, are not entitled to such support.

Added to this, public educational institutions are in practice often given considerable autonomy and act as independent or semi-independent quasi-autonomous non-governmental organisations (quangos). Ancient universities, for instance, often have longstanding legal protections in their statutes that give them some degree of freedom from the state. In other words, the public role can be complex with the main responsibilities sometimes lying not with the government, but with some other body accountable to it. In the running of schools, for example, headteachers often have a substantial influence about how their school is run, but they often also have to answer to their own school governing body that may include some parents and local politicians in their membership. Representatives of other groups interested in education – such as teachers, religious bodies or sometimes even businesses – are also often granted the right to participate in different ways.

For the most part, public education institutions are funded through general taxation. However, recent concerns about the cost of education have led to increased use of co-payments: that is, charges to individual students, usually in the form of tuition fees. This is particularly so for tertiary education, but in many lower-income countries it is also true for other levels of education. How tuition fees themselves are gathered varies somewhat from place to place. While some countries ask for upfront payment of fees in cash – which students may have to borrow from family or commercial organisations – many countries either provide the necessary money in the form of a government-funded student loan that is paid back after graduation (often at a favourable rate of interest and only after the student earns a certain level of income) or the money is collected after graduation via a special graduate tax. In some countries, these loans cover living costs as well as tuition fee payments.

Aside from the issues surrounding financing and the formal ownership of educational institutions, education systems can differ considerably in how they organise schooling and a contrast can be drawn between *unitary (comprehensive) systems of schooling* that emphasise common schooling independent from an individual pupil's attainment and systems in which *academic selection* underpins the *specialisation and stratification of schooling* rather than a common education.

The Swedish education system provides a good example of a unitary system. Here, all young people are taught in comprehensive schools up to the age of 16 and the unitary character of the school system is also retained during the upper-secondary level. Only in higher education do we find some disparities as young people are able to choose between a professional qualification (university diploma) and a variety of general degrees (diploma, bachelor, masters). Sweden is thus similar to other Scandinavian countries (such as Denmark) in which academic selection – and therefore some degree of educational segregation – is institutionalised at a rather late point of individual educational careers. At the same time, this pattern is by no means exclusive to Scandinavian countries. For instance, Japan shows a similar structure of the education systems, albeit selection commencing at upper-secondary level and therefore slightly earlier.

By contrast, Germany has been identified as a prime example of a selective education system. Here pupils are divided into different types of school as early as the ages of 11 to 12 years old. Some unitary schools exist in Germany, but pupils normally go on to learn in so-called *Hauptschulen, Realschulen* or *Gymnasiums*, largely depending on their attainment in primary education. Pupils can receive a first general education qualification after nine years in the *Hauptschule* or a secondary school-level certificate (sometimes called an O-level) after 10th grade in the *Realschule*. Both of these certificates normally lead to some form of upper-secondary education in vocational schools or on-the-job training in the so-called 'dual system' in which young people spend their time both in vocational schools and also working for their (potential) future employers at the same time. The *Gymnasium* is the typical route for those aspiring to an A-level certificate that is typically followed by enrolment into higher education with one of the many different (poly-)technical, pedagogic and arts colleges or universities. In short, rather different educational routes are put in place for different groups of pupils at a very early stage of their educational careers.

There are other important variations in how nations organise schooling that it is worth shedding some light on. For instance, we might want to look at the length of education – or overall **school life expectancy** – that is typical for each nation. As we can see from Table 4.2, the actual age at which the majority of young people leave the education system varies considerably across countries. Turkey and Mexico, appear to be most 'unequal' in our small sample as about 60% of the 15- to 19-year-olds were no longer enrolled in the education system in 2004. Only about 10% of all young people in their twenties had the chance to study at tertiary level in these countries. Of all the countries included in Table 4.2, only Indonesia shows a similar pattern of educational transition. The vast majority of countries for which such data are available keep their young people in education until they reach the ages of 18 and 19. Among the

Table 4.2: Educational participation (full-time and part-time students in public and private institutions as % of population in age group, from age 3-4 to age 20-29), 2003/04

	Age			
	3-4	5-14	15-19	20-29
Argentina	41.2	100	69.0	25.7
Australia	42.4	98.5	81.6	32.6
China	13.3	88.7	–	–
Czech Republic	84.3	99.7	91.4	18.6
Denmark	87.6	98.0	84.5	36.0
France	100	100	87.1	20.8
Germany	76.9	97.9	88.8	27.9
Indonesia	–	89.3	54.4	4.0
Italy	100	100	78.8	19.4
Korea	20.3	93.5	85.2	27.4
Mexico	44.5	97.7	41.6	10.0
Netherlands	36.6	99.6	86.1	25.5
Philippines	–	79.2	60.9	–
Poland	32.2	94.5	89.8	30.2
Sweden	85.1	99.1	87.5	35.8
Turkey	2.6	81.2	39.8	9.6
United Kingdom	76.7	100	79.0	27.8
United States	52.9	97.3	76.5	23.4
Uruguay	23.0	97.5	64.0	16.5

Source: Adapted from UNESCO/OECD (2007)

high-income countries, Italy, the UK and the US are an exception as rates drop to a comparatively low 70% for 15- to 19-year-olds. Conversely, in Denmark and Sweden, 35% or more of their 20- to 29-year-olds remain in either upper-secondary or tertiary education.

Another way of approaching the typical length of education in a country is to examine the working-age population by their *highest level of educational attainment*; this indicator does not emphasise total years in education, but the highest achieved certificate and the two do not necessarily have to correspond. Table 4.3 shows that no or only incomplete primary schooling is – statistically speaking – no longer a major issue for virtually all high-income countries. At the same time, the percentages of the total population falling under this category in 2003/04 are staggering in some countries. For instance, 45% of the total adult population in Thailand did not complete primary education and the figures for several other middle- and low-income countries are equally high (see Box 4.2).

Box 4.2	Obstacles to higher primary school enrolment in middle- and low-income countries

The development of basic education in middle- and low-income countries has been at the forefront of initiatives for sustainable development and the delivery of essential human rights for a long time now. While progress has been impressive – helped by large sums of money invested by both national governments and international aid – education opportunity is still lacking in some countries. The reasons for this are many. Below are some of those typically identified in the academic literature:

■ Parents are in many cases exposed to a decision about the 'opportunity costs' of schooling – that is, they have to evaluate the cost of sending their child to school and compare this with the child's expected future income. Direct costs to consider are those for school uniforms, books, tuition fees and so on. The loss of a potential source of income or the loss of the child's support for family or farm work is also an important factor.

■ Male and female differentials in literacy and school enrolment are substantial in many middle- and low-income countries. Cultural and religious attitudes towards women's role in society can play a crucial role here. Education is one of the primary means of gaining access into formal employment. At the same time, access to formal employment is often limited for women, which for many families does not make their education seem worthwhile.

- The relevance of education programmes is not always a given for males as well. Attempts to emulate approaches in high-income countries may come at the cost of disregarding local economic realities and the lack of certain employment opportunities.

- The quality of many schools is still poor. Inadequate support and the poor qualification of teachers are blamed for comparably high rates of repetition of classes and for high numbers of dropouts. The high numbers of repeaters is conducive to overcrowding of classes, thus spurring a vicious circle and increasing the risk for parents who consider sending their child to school.

- According to calculations by UNESCO, many middle- and low-income countries will continue to depend on international aid to extend basic education programmes for many years. The dependency on external donors may favour short- over long-term policy programmes to increase the reach of basic education.

As for countries within the OECD, the percentages of the adult population completing primary, lower-secondary and upper-secondary education still show a great deal of variety. In the most educated nations around 50% of the adult population completed upper-secondary education and around 30% obtained one of the many available tertiary certificates (see, in Table 4.3, Canada, Denmark, Germany, Japan, South Korea, Netherlands, Sweden, the UK and the US, for example). Russia is the only non-OECD country that reached similar levels in 2003/04.

A separate look at tertiary education is interesting as it shows that several OECD countries seem to be lagging behind. Canada had the highest tertiary completion rate of the adult population in 2003/04

Table 4.3: **Educational attainment of the adult population, 2003/04 (%)[a]**

	No or incomplete schooling	Primary	Lower secondary	Upper secondary	Tertiary
Argentina	10	34	14	28	14
Australia	0	0	36	33	31
Belgium	0	16	19	34	30
Brazil	28	28	14	22	8
Canada	0	5	11	40	44
Chile	13	11	26	37	13
Denmark	0	1	15	51	32
Finland	0	13	10	43	34
France	0	15	20	41	24
Germany	0	2	14	60	25
Indonesia	19	39	18	19	4
Italy	0	19	32	38	11
Japan	0	0	16	47	38
Mexico	0	51	26	6	16
Netherlands	0	8	21	42	29
Paraguay	34	31	11	16	8
Philippines	18	18	13	24	27
South Korea	0	13	13	44	30
Spain	0	28	27	19	26
Sweden	0	7	10	48	34
Thailand	45	22	11	10	12
United Kingdom	0	–	15	55	29
United States	0	5	8	49	39

Note: [a] Distribution of the population aged 25-64 years, by highest level of education attained.

Source: UNESCO/OECD (2007)

followed by the US, Japan, Finland and Sweden. In all of these countries more than a third of the adult population completed tertiary education. In contrast, France, Germany, Spain and particularly Italy had noticeably lower rates. Education systems in these countries have come under some criticism for not expanding the numbers of students in higher education in recent years. Some analysts have taken these figures as proof that the according education systems have not adapted adequately to the challenges of globalisation and the emerging 'knowledge economies'.

A large part of the reluctance to expand higher education may be a result of the very costly nature of highly specialised tertiary education. Indeed, a growing trend within the OECD has been for governments to share the cost of higher education with students themselves, most notably by charging tuition fees. Significantly, these fees vary substantially across countries: some countries do not have tuition fees for full-time students at all; others do not have them for public, but for private institutions; finally, in some countries students have to pay irrespective of whether they go to a public or private institution. Where they do exist, annual average tuition fees for public institutions range from below US$500 in countries like Belgium, Hungary and Turkey to up to well over US$3,000 in Canada, Japan, Korea and Chile. In Australia and the US tuition fees reached between US$4,500 and US$5,200 on average in the academic year 2003/04. While some of these figures appear extraordinary, tuition fees in private institutions are generally higher and go up to an average of US$18,000 in the US. (We should note that the term *average* needs to be properly understood here, for the levels of the top end in the US are well in excess of this US$18,000 figure.) Naturally, a representation of tertiary education without considering that students may receive scholarships or grants in support of the tuition fees or living costs is somewhat incomplete. In fact, for the majority of countries for which data are available we find that between 70% and 80% of the home student body is supported financially; these are figures for public sector institutions – the corresponding rates for private institutions are mostly closer to 80% and 100%.

Key policy issues

An individual's education is among the main determinants of both working careers and unemployment across the high-income countries and the importance of educational qualifications has been heightened with the emergence of **knowledge economies**. Historically, lower-skilled workers have shared in the overall growth in affluence during much of the post-war period by receiving relatively generous wage increases and maintaining relatively secure work contracts. Broader changes in industrial production have resulted in many industrial jobs becoming redundant (see also Chapter Three) and so the percentage of the labour force employed in the agricultural and industrial sector has decreased from just above 50% in 1960 to merely about 25% in the OECD countries. As a consequence, individuals with low skills, who in the past would have found a stable 'haven' in these sectors, often have to be content with low-paid, often precarious jobs in the service industry. This is certainly a somewhat simplified version of nearly 60 years of progression in political economies. However, some figures may help to underline the significance of these changes.

For instance, the percentage of low-qualified people without completed vocational training among long-term unemployed people is exceptionally high in Germany. The specific unemployment rate for university and technical college graduates has been below 4% throughout the past 25 years. At the same time, the proportion of unemployed people without completed vocational training has more than doubled to just below 25%. In other words, the risk of employees without high levels of education or advanced vocational training being permanently excluded from the labour market is higher than ever before. This pattern of unemployment risk is a particular issue in Germany but by no means unique in this country. In 2004, the average unemployment rate for individuals with only lower-secondary education was close to 11% across the OECD, while the rate for those with a tertiary degree was merely 4% at the same time. Such gaps appeared to be particularly pronounced in nations with educational systems that instituted a strong and early division between academic and vocational education of young people, but so-called **skill-biased technological change** – a shift in rewards of employment that favours those with very specialised skills in the new knowledge-based economy – has been identified by economists as a major factor in explaining rising income inequality in OECD nations.

Indeed, Figure 4.2 illustrates that educational attainment has a substantial impact on individual earnings. In all of the countries in the chart we can see that those whose formal education finished at the upper-secondary school level or below are much more likely to be in poverty (defined as earning at or below half of the median income) than those who complete tertiary education. Contrarily, those who graduate at the tertiary level are much more likely to be on very high incomes (more than two times the median). This last point has also been made in the economics literature for some time now. Cross-national research in this field has uncovered striking relationships between the total number of school years and the wage levels of the working population, with those looking back at relatively short careers in education finding themselves in the growing low-paid sector of the labour market.

We should not, however, presume that more education is necessarily an effective route for tackling poverty and inequality. Indeed, while some hail education as the most important component of social policy in the 21st century, there is much to suggest that education can actually play

Figure 4.2: Poverty and educational attainment, 2004/05

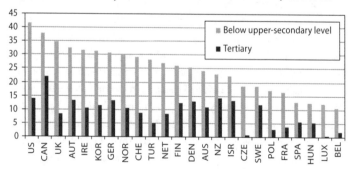

Notes: Percentage of population aged between 25 and 64 living at below half median earnings with highest educational attainment of (a) below upper-secondary level and (b) tertiary level.

Source: OECD (2007b)

a role in increasing social divisions. This is likely to be particularly so if educational opportunities are not equally available to all or if the benefits of education are more likely to be accrued by the already better-off and, for the most part, this seems to be so. Indeed, a recent cross-national analysis of educational attainment in OECD countries (the Programme for International Student Assessment – PISA) found that in some countries there were significant variations in the performance of schools and, more importantly, that much of this variation could be accounted for by the different socioeconomic backgrounds of the pupils within those schools (see Figure 4.3). Or, put more simply, in many countries there seems to be a clear social stratification of schooling, with better-off pupils attending better-achieving school, suggesting that equality of opportunity is far from being a reality in most OECD countries. Importantly, the countries in which this kind of stratification was minimised were primarily those in which a unitary (or comprehensive) model of education exists. Similar evidence is emerging with respect to social mobility, recent data showing that the Scandinavian nations have much higher levels of mobility than the US, the UK and Germany. In the UK, moreover, there is strong evidence to suggest that social mobility has actually declined in recent years partially because of the strong link between parental income and a child's educational attainment (see Box 4.3).

Figure 4.3: Variance between schools in students' performance in mathematics[a]

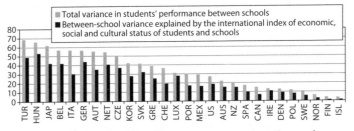

Note: [a] Expressed as a percentage of the average variance in student performance in OECD countries.

Source: OECD (2003)

Box 4.3	Education and declining social mobility in the UK

We should be wary of presuming that education always acts as a tool for enhancing social mobility or promoting equality of opportunity. Indeed, recent evidence from the UK has pointed to the significant role education has played in *reducing* the level of social mobility there in recent years (Blanden et al, 2005).

Comparing people born in 1958 with those born in 1970, the researchers found that for the latter group, earnings at age 30 were more closely tied with their parents' earnings during childhood than was the case for those born in 1958. Or, in other words, their position in the income 'hierarchy' was more heavily influenced by their parents' position within it than had been the case for an earlier generation. Equality of opportunity had become less of a reality for the children of 1970 than for the children of 1958.

The researchers explored reasons for this decline in social mobility and education was found to explain a large part of this change, not least because a child's educational attainment had become more heavily tied to their parents' income. While they found that educational attainment – measured in terms of completion rates at different stages of education – had improved considerably for those from low-income households during this period, so too had the educational attainment of those from high-income households. Crucially, the attainment of the latter had increased more rapidly than that of the former.

Significantly, the starkest differences appeared to be at the tertiary education stage. While the numbers attending university from all social backgrounds had increased over time, the researchers found that the better-off had gained much more from the expansion of tertiary education. Moreover, they surmised that the extension of co-payments in the form of student loans and tuition fees was likely to have played a key role in tying the completion of a university degree much more tightly to parental income for the children of 1970 in comparison with the children of 1958.

We should note, however, that the researchers found little evidence of a similarly strong link in the US or the Scandinavian countries: rather than being a general trend, the situation in the UK appears to be an outcome of the specifics of this case.

From a macroeconomic perspective, numerous international organisations have emphasised the relationship between education and economic growth. Some scholars have shown that gross secondary school enrolment across the high- and low-income countries is positively correlated with annual growth rates of GDP – that is, those countries which achieved higher rates of secondary school enrolment since the 1960s have consistently done better in terms of their economic performance compared to those with comparatively lower levels. Similar patterns have been uncovered for the relationship between economic growth and education spending. The argument that education delivers growth is thereby based on the fundamental assumption that economically advanced, productive nations are in need of a lot of educated individuals. Also, technological progress is said to rely on innovations from top-class universities and research laboratories. South Korea and Singapore are commonly presented as prime examples of countries in which governments have intervened massively in education policy and in which economic growth rates have surpassed those of many of their competitors since the early 1980s.

However, the relationship between school enrolment and economic growth is not deterministic and we should be wary of presenting education as a 'magic bullet' for economic policy. If we only concentrate on the high-income countries of the OECD, for instance, the clear link between educational attainment and economic performance found in some research becomes less straightforward: in fact the evidence shows that numerous OECD countries deviate from this pattern of high education spending producing high economic growth. Among the middle- and low-income countries similar problematic cases can be found and scholars have underlined that not all 'Asian tigers' have invested heavily in education in the way South Korea or Singapore did, yet they still achieved similar economic growth rates (for example, Hong Kong and China). Other countries around the world have made similar attempts to expand the overall educational attainment of their labour force without gaining significant economic progress (for example, Egypt and Sri Lanka).

Unfortunately, even if we put economic considerations to one side and focus purely on academic concerns, the relationship between investment in education systems and educational and economic outcomes is far from straightforward. The recent PISA study mentioned above found that, for instance, neither public nor private school spending is directly correlated with the pupils' proficiency levels in mathematics. In part this may be because, as a labour-intensive service, much of the spending goes directly on teachers' salaries; the overall level of spending tells us little about the quality of education in terms of class sizes or the standard of equipment within schools, for instance. For governments increasing investment in education, therefore, there are tricky questions to be tackled about how to best guarantee a return on this investment.

Yet despite the lack of clear evidence about the impact of educational expansion, most countries have looked to extend educational opportunities in recent years. Plans to increase the number of school leavers continuing their education at the tertiary level, along with innovative programmes of lifelong learning and access programmes for mature students as well as increased numbers of student migrants have increased university student numbers in many countries. Simultaneously, the importance of early childhood education has gained increased attention in many places with some countries adopting more generous child benefit programmes and expanding the availability of day nurseries and pre-schools. All of the above necessitates further investments in the education system. Indeed, the majority of governments around the globe currently share the commitment to increase education spending to train and hire more skilled teachers as well as to build, improve and modernise existing schools and universities.

All this, of course, raises questions about how to finance this expansion and the introduction of – or the increase in the level of – co-payments in education has been a commonly used solution. Most notably, many OECD countries have introduced or increased the level of tuition fee payments in higher education, but some commentators have expressed worries about the fact that many students have been forced to accumulate considerable amounts of debts at the start of their young working careers. Proponents of tuition fees argue that the additional funds are necessary to attract leading teachers and researchers in highly specialised fields and to improve student/teacher ratios as well as the quality of and access to libraries and other student resources. By pointing to countries such as the US, Canada and South Korea, in which relatively high tuition fees have been paired with high and rapidly increasing tertiary education participation rates for some time now, proponents of fee charging argue that co-payments can be compatible with expanding access to higher education. Yet there is some evidence that suggests that when tuition fees are not accompanied by wide-ranging and generous scholarship programmes those from lower-income backgrounds are often discouraged from studying at the tertiary level, thus decreasing social diversity in universities (and threatening social mobility) even further. Moreover, there is evidence that the level of fees may also be crucial: in Australia, for instance, the levying of fees appeared to have been successful in expanding access without threatening diversity, but more recent increases in fee levels seem to have changed the picture somewhat.

At the heart of these debates – and this is where we are going full circle and return to the beginning of this chapter – is a major question about the fundamental goals of the education system. Countries with relatively high percentages of private spending in tertiary education typically feature a higher dispersion of teaching quality and student attainment. From a human capital perspective this may be very desirable. For instance, it can be argued that having a small number of very well-funded elite universities not only produces elite students (sometimes referred to as high achievers), but also has an important role to play in national strategies for producing specialised, cutting-edge research and development that in turn leads to the new patents, products, ideas and technologies that bring success in the competitive global knowledge economy. To this end, some countries have in fact encouraged a stratification of the university sector by allowing universities to charge variable fees on the basis of a presumed variation in the quality of the institutions themselves. This is partly a response to the very high costs of maintaining a world-leading research university, but it is also a strategy that is based on the presumption that some people are more able than others. Reconciling an equitable model education with one that develops the talents of elite scholars is a far from easy task.

SUMMARY

■ Education can play a key role in promoting **social cohesion** and **social mobility**.
■ It can be **selective** or **unitary**.
■ It has different functions at the **primary**, **secondary** and **tertiary** levels.
■ Education is deemed to be an increasingly important **economic tool**.
■ It plays a central role in shaping a nation's **human capital**.
■ It can help boost individuals' **financial rewards**.
■ It can contribute to **inequality** and **decreasing social mobility**.

READING GUIDE

Tomlinson (2005) provides a detailed historical account of how the significance of education policy has changed since the 1950s. Unfortunately, her discussion is solely focused on the British case and is thus not very helpful for those who are interested in a more international perspective. Such an international perspective is adopted by Olssen and his colleagues (2004) as they discuss the impact of education in the global economy with references to the 'post-structuralism' of the French philosopher

Michel Foucault. However, if you are not prepared to engage with an intriguing, but nevertheless highly theoretical and somewhat abstract debate, this is probably not the book for you either. More helpful might be Crouch et al's (1999) contribution in which they focus on methods of training and skills creation across high-income countries to study how these have reacted to the challenges of the emerging 'knowledge economies' and whether the adapted policy strategies are sufficient to tackle these. Castles' (2007) wider discussion on the functions of states in the 21st century as they try to defend themselves against the global and economic pressures of retrenchment also contains several references to the changing role of education as an economic and social development strategy.

The statistics used in this chapter were taken from several sources that are all available to interested readers on the internet. Human Development Statistics published by the United Nations Development Project (UNDP) contain data on public and private investment in education for virtually all nations around the globe (www.undp.org/). UNESCO has published a much wider range of information on international education systems in its World Education Indicators database (www.uis.unesco.org/ev_en.php?ID=5263_201&ID2=DO_TOPIC). Statistics on finance, investment, enrolment and, to some extent, attainment can all be found on this site. The sample of countries in this database is not restricted to high-income nations, but includes several non-OECD nations: Argentina, Brazil, Chile, China, Egypt, India, Indonesia, Jamaica, Jordan, Malaysia, Paraguay, Peru, the Philippines, the Russian Federation, Sri Lanka, Thailand, Tunisia, Uruguay and Zimbabwe. The most detailed data on the functioning of education systems is still published in the OECD *Education at a glance* reports. The statistics used to inform these period reports – including the latest findings of the latest PISA studies – are obtainable from the official OECD webpage (www.oecd.org).

5

health

Introduction

Healthcare is unquestionably one of the major fields of public and social policy and it is often at the heart of political debate. There are obvious reasons for this, not least the fact that access to healthcare services is vital for our general well-being. Indeed, it is central to our basic human rights – including the right to life – and Article 25 of the *Universal Declaration of Human Rights* (UN Assembly, 1948) states that both access to medical care and, more generally, a standard of living adequate for health and well-being are fundamental rights.

Yet despite such acceptance of the importance of healthcare services, in most countries there is a vigorous debate about the shortcomings and shortfalls of healthcare provision. In part this is a consequence of the huge potential of modern medicine: continual scientific advances lead to new diagnoses, treatments and interventions and the financial cost of providing all citizens with unlimited and unrestricted access to the full range of healthcare interventions is beyond even the richest of countries (see Box 5.1). In other words, **rationing** is a feature of healthcare systems. However, it should also be noted that the organisation of healthcare systems fundamentally shapes who has access to services that are provided. Indeed, inequalities of access are a feature of most healthcare systems and such inequities often form the focal point of debate.

Box 5.1	Ever-expanding demand?

In the early days of state expansion into healthcare, it was believed by some that as access to health services expanded the level of ill-health in society would drop and so, therefore, would demand for (and the cost of) healthcare provision. This view proved to be deeply flawed and, despite recent concerns with cost containment, healthcare expenditure has expanded in countries with well-developed health systems. There are many reasons that this is so, but two in particular are worthy of note: *technological advancement* and *population ageing*.

The sheer scale of modern medicine brings more rapid advances in knowledge than was previously the case. New treatments and procedures are developed with regularity and, indeed, our ability to diagnose medical conditions also expands. While not all advances will increase spending – many, in fact, save money by improving on existing treatments – there is a consensus that overall they have contributed heavily to increasing healthcare costs and certainly it is difficult for government to deny citizens access to new treatments as they become available.

A large part of the costs of technological advancement are indirect: by contributing to our ability to extend life expectancy, medical advances have been one of the causes of the ageing of populations in high-income countries. However, a concern for policy makers is that the average healthcare costs of those aged 65 and over are higher than those for the rest of the population, with some estimates suggesting that they are three to four times greater.

Of course, advances in medical technology and increased life expectancies are very important health policy success stories, so we should avoid dubbing these issues as 'problems' as some people tend to do. Indeed, both may bring greater costs to healthcare systems, but most would agree that these costs are more than balanced by the enormous benefits they bring.

Healthcare policy is typically thought of in terms of medical services delivered by doctors and nurses in hospitals or community health facilities such as clinics or doctors' surgeries. Such activities are at the heart of healthcare policy, and will form the core of this chapter, but a broader definition would also encompass the services provided by dentists, opticians and pharmacists and arguably those of medical research scientists too. It might also include the delivery of measures that aim to tackle particular health-related problems (such as obesity or alcohol abuse) through health promotion programmes or involve planning for potential health hazards and pandemics (such as the outbreak of bird flu). It could encompass attempts to tackle healthcare inequalities such as varying life expectancy rates across a nation through programmes that involve addressing a wide range of underlying issues that affect our physical and mental well-being such as housing conditions, the quality of the local environment and the distribution of income in society.

The scale and importance of healthcare policies can be illustrated by pointing to their cost (see Table 5.1). In high-income countries, spending by the government in this area typically accounts for between 6% and 9% of GDP. Even in less wealthy countries expenditure between 4% and 7% of GDP is not uncommon, although there are many places where expenditure is only around 1% or 2% of GDP. Added to this mix, however, are often very substantial levels of private spending on healthcare. Indeed, in some countries – such as the US – private spending exceeds public spending. When both public and private spending is accounted for many high-income countries allocate in excess of 10% of their GDP to healthcare. In short, healthcare is big business in most countries.

Key policy goals

At the most basic level, the goal of healthcare policy can be defined as ensuring that citizens have access to adequate medical provision. More often than not this will be during times of ill-health but medical services are often required as a matter of routine by those who are perfectly healthy (for example, during childbirth or vaccination). What is deemed adequate medical provision – and how states grant access

Table 5.1: Healthcare expenditure (as % of GDP), 2004			
	Public spending	Private spending	Public and private
High-income countries			
United States	6.9	8.5	15.4
Germany	8.2	2.4	10.6
France	8.2	2.3	10.5
Norway	8.1	1.6	9.7
United Kingdom	7.0	1.1	8.1
Upper middle-income countries			
Costa Rica	5.1	1.5	6.6
Russian Federation	3.7	2.3	6.0
Mauritius	2.4	1.9	4.3
Lower middle-income countries			
El Salvador	3.5	4.4	7.9
Maldives	6.3	1.4	7.7
Iran (Islamic Republic of)	3.2	3.4	6.6
Lesotho	5.5	1.0	6.5
Low-income countries			
Mongolia	4.0	2.0	6.0
Vietnam	1.5	4.0	5.5
Bhutan	3.0	1.6	4.6
Source: UNDP (2007)			

– varies considerably between nations, however. Indeed, these variations are often quite stark.

In many countries, the state is the main provider of healthcare services and, in most high-income countries, has played a very large role for much of the past 100 years. The expansion of state involvement in healthcare has complex roots, but typically it was in response to the high cost of healthcare provided by the free market, and the subsequent threat to well-being that arose from a widespread lack of access to medical services, that the state expanded its role in the provision of health services. Indeed, economists often point to healthcare as a classic example of market failure as many of those who are in greatest need of medical assistance are those who are least likely to be able to afford it, not least because disease and ill-health hamper an individual's ability to earn money through employment (Glennerster, 2003). However, the expansion of state involvement has taken many different forms. We will examine the detail of the different mechanisms in the next section of this chapter, but generally speaking three 'ideal types' can be seen in the high-income countries, each with slightly differing goals.

First, there are those nations where the state plays the dominant role in healthcare by acting as a near monopoly supplier of health services. In these cases, the state owns the majority of healthcare facilities such as hospitals and clinics, employs the majority of medical professionals and funds services directly through taxes. Typically, because the service is funded through taxation, all citizens are entitled to use the service on the basis of need, not the ability to pay: in other words, there is universal service provision. Such systems view the provision of healthcare as a government or public responsibility and the high levels of public provision crowd out private services, although a modestly sized private sector typically co-exists alongside the state system. The universal principles underpinning these systems offer a service that delivers relatively equal access to healthcare and they can be viewed as broadly egalitarian in intent. Systems of this sort exist in the UK and in Sweden and can be broadly dubbed as *social democratic* systems.

At the other extreme are countries where healthcare is primarily seen as private responsibility and therefore a matter for the free market. In such cases, individuals in need of treatment will typically receive it in privately owned hospitals and clinics and will be charged for the cost of so doing; patients can cover these costs either by using their own private medical insurance – sometimes provided as part of an employment package – or by paying one-off fees from their own pocket. Consequently, access is determined on the basis of ability to pay: if a citizen cannot afford to pay the fee or does not have insurance to cover the cost then they will not receive treatment. However, in these cases the private market is typically supported by a state-organised healthcare **safety net**. This can take many forms, but often involves the provision of state-organised emergency services to cover unplanned treatments (for example, those resulting from accidents) and a state-organised insurance scheme that provides funds for those on low incomes who cannot cover the costs of care themselves or whose insurance scheme will not meet the full costs of treatment. In such instances, public support is usually provided on a means-tested basis: it is available only to those deemed unable to afford the full cost of private cover. The underpinning values of these systems are almost the polar opposite of the social democratic system we described above. The state aims to stimulate private provision rather than to crowd it out; indeed the state's rule is limited to that of provider of last resort in order to facilitate this and, moreover, equity is not a core concern for the system because major inequities in access necessarily arise when the free market determines what is provided. These systems can be broadly dubbed as *liberal* systems and the US is a good example of such an approach.

A third option is almost a middle way between the two systems described above and involves the state organising a comprehensive social health insurance fund that collects a fixed percentage of all citizens' income via the taxation system. These social insurance schemes are designed to cover the costs of medical treatments incurred by citizens, but the provision of services themselves is often left to the private, voluntary and quasi-governmental sectors, making the system much more sympathetic towards the development of a private health services market than the social democratic model. This differs from the private insurance approach in so far as it allows for a collective pooling of funds so that all citizens can be covered and all pay an equal share of their income. Moreover, because payments are collected through the taxation system, membership of a scheme is compulsory rather than a matter of individual choice. The social insurance/private insurance distinction may seem a fine-grained one, but is hugely important in practice because the two systems have rather different goals. Unlike private insurance schemes, social insurance-based schemes emphasise the need for universal coverage of healthcare services and so have some degree of equity built within them. Indeed, they insure against collective risks rather than individual risks. However, unlike the social democratic schemes, greater variation in the nature of service is sometimes permitted because the state's role is limited to the collection of finance. Indeed, some countries allow citizens a choice between different competing social insurance funds, each with different terms of service. As with the social democratic system, there is usually a modestly sized private insurance sector that allows those with higher incomes to join schemes that offer additional levels of protection. This system might be broadly dubbed a corporatist system and Germany and France have systems like this.

This three-way division has strong parallels to that found in the social security sector (see Chapter Two) and, just as Esping-Andersen (1990) argued that there were three worlds of welfare in the field of social security, some have suggested that there are also three worlds of healthcare (Bambra, 2005), so we have used the same labels for the three systems here. In practice, as we noted above, in most nations public and private sector services co-exist; in other words, most nations offer a **mixed economy** of provision. However, the state's role varies greatly from that of main provider of healthcare to merely the funder of a last-resort safety net, a fact reflected in the differing spending patterns shown in Table 5.1.

Key delivery mechanisms

In examining the key delivery mechanisms in the healthcare sector, it makes sense to break the discussion into two distinct parts: one dealing with *service funding* mechanisms and the other dealing with *service provision* mechanisms. As indicated in the previous section, the state influences both these dimensions of healthcare, although different countries can adopt quite different roles in each. We will begin our discussion by looking at funding mechanisms before going on to look at service provision.

The most basic of service funding mechanisms is for governments to simply use general taxation to fund healthcare policies. In such instances, the government does not establish any special funds to cover the cost of health services or ask citizens to make any specially differentiated tax or social insurance payments towards health services; instead, the government merely treats healthcare as one of many different policy areas competing for a share of its regular tax revenues. Such an approach gives the government a great degree of flexibility over the allocation of funds, allowing it to increase or decrease the amount of monies allocated to the health budget without having to make special adjustments to dedicated healthcare taxes. It also allows the government to easily move funds between different areas of policy if priorities change without, for instance, explaining why it wants to remove surplus funds from a dedicated national healthcare account. This, of course, is not necessarily a strength of the approach: it certainly has the potential to politicise health spending and can make it easy for a hostile government to restrict funding of health services. On the other hand, it also makes it easy for a sympathetic government to expand funding. For the most part, this is how the UK's NHS is funded.

However, in many nations there are tighter restrictions on the state's control over healthcare funds. Indeed, in much of Western Europe services are funded by dedicated social health insurance funds. In such cases, a proportion of a citizen's earnings must be paid into a health insurance fund (in Germany, for example, an average of 7.55% of earnings was paid into these funds in 2006, albeit with some variations for those on very low or high incomes), with the state and the citizen's employer usually making a contribution too. Although in effect a form of taxation – contributions have to be made by law and the government usually sets the contribution levels as part of its regular budgeting process – the allocation of these funds is not usually at the discretion of the government because the contributions have been earmarked for healthcare expenditure. Indeed, in some countries the funds are managed by non-governmental agencies. While the loss of flexibility in such systems is sometimes bemoaned, there are advantages to such an approach, not least the fact that citizens can see where a substantial part of their tax payments are being directed: for a government looking to increase welfare expenditure, a proposed rise in social health insurance contributions is usually much less likely to cause a political stir than a rise in the general rate of taxation because people can see a clear link between their increased contribution and actual service provision.

These first two mechanisms are collective or social mechanisms: that is, they involve raising compulsory payments from the public using the government's tax-raising powers. On top of these public forms of funding, most countries also rely on considerable private financing of health services. First, *private health insurance* has a wide base in many countries. For-profit and not-for-profit schemes operate in almost every country in the world. As noted above, these schemes vary in terms of their market penetration. For instance, in 2005, private health insurance schemes provided 37% of healthcare finance in the US, but in Denmark they were the source of only 1.5% of healthcare spending (OECD, 2007c). Private health insurance schemes are, in principle, similar to insurance products of any other sort: individual customers pay regular premiums to an insurer in return for coverage against major healthcare risks. As with all insurance products, premiums vary according to the individual customer's exposure to risk and the level of coverage offered by competing insurers can vary quite widely. Indeed, both the main advantage and disadvantage of private insurance is the more personalised service it offers: relatively healthy people deemed 'good risks' by the insurers may be offered favourable terms of service including lower premiums but, conversely, those with a poor health record or long-term illness may find their premiums significantly more expensive on average. In many countries private insurance schemes act primarily as a supplement to widespread publicly funded healthcare services and, in such cases, the main incentive for individuals to join a private health insurance scheme is usually that it offers a marginal service enhancement such as more choice over when treatment is offered or greater speed of access to services.

In addition to private insurance schemes, *one-off charges* or *user payments* are another important private finance mechanism, be they for surgical procedures, prescription medicines or consultations with medical professionals. These charges can be for access to public services as well as for private ones: in Germany, for instance, a €10 payment is required for the first visit to a general practitioner in each quarter, a cost that cannot be recouped from social health insurance funds. More common still are charges for non-medical costs that may nonetheless inevitably be incurred during the course of treatment: meals eaten during a stay in hospital for instance.

We should also make it clear that there is often a real blurring of boundaries between public and private funding in practice. As noted above, in many countries citizens are covered by a patchwork of public and private schemes. Most notably, while contributions to private health insurance funds may appear to be a candidate for a purely private funding source, in practice many countries offer tax breaks or tax subsidies on private health insurance contributions: because these tax breaks involve the loss of potential tax revenue they are, in effect, forms of negative government spending. While this may seem a somewhat obscure argument, it should be borne in mind that such subsidies are active government policies, usually introduced to stimulate the take-up of private health insurance. In Australia, for instance, the government provides a 30% subsidy to individual private health insurance payments specifically because it believes that expanding private involvement in healthcare provision is to the benefit of the Australian healthcare system as a whole (OECD, 2004).

The complex interweaving of public and private service funding mechanisms in most countries is usually matched by a similarly complex interweaving of public and private service delivery mechanisms. Once again, perhaps the most straightforward mechanism – conceptually at least – comes in the form of state ownership of medical facilities such as hospitals and clinics. In some countries the state is the main supplier of medical services of this sort, being responsible for the building, staffing and management of key healthcare institutions.

While state ownership stills forms the backbone of the health service in many countries, even those with a large state sector tend to possess a more complex pattern of public provision in practice. For instance, public hospitals are often placed under the ownership of independent or semi-independent quangos or, indeed, are quangos in their own right. In the UK, for instance, some public hospitals have been allowed to become 'foundation hospitals', giving them greater autonomy in planning budgets and staffing, including the power to borrow money independently of the government. Added to this, even when the state does supply staff and manage health facilities, it may often finance the building or purchasing of such facilities through money borrowed from private sources. Indeed, in some countries it is not uncommon for the state to lease large buildings from private companies. Similarly, much of the equipment and medical supplies on which health services rely are usually provided by private corporations. Indeed, it is worth noting that the pharmaceuticals market, for instance, is increasingly dominated by a small number of very powerful multinational corporations on whom states depend for the supply of key medications. The power of these corporations can be a particularly acute problem for governments in low-income countries (see Box 5.2).

Box 5.2 The challenges of delivering equitable healthcare in South Africa

The structure of the South African healthcare system has complex roots that emanate from its recent history and, in particular, its transition from a racist apartheid regime to a modern democracy. During much of the apartheid era, healthcare policy itself was racist, with separate medical facilities existing for white and black people and funding allocations often unfairly distributed, but in the run-up to the democratic transition in 1994, policy changed and medical services were desegregated. In the period since, significant healthcare reforms have been introduced in order to improve the funding of public services and expand access to healthcare facilities with the underlying goal of making healthcare more equitable.

However, the reforms have been far from successful in equalising access (see Committee of Inquiry into a Comprehensive System of Social Security, 2002). Indeed, while significant strides towards a universal public health service have been made, in practice significant inequities remain. In particular, because the higher-quality hospitals were already located in white neighbourhoods, an informal geographic barrier to access persists, with many of the best facilities inaccessible or less accessible to many black people. Moreover, public hospitals and clinics are of good quality but overstretched and waiting times can be long. Perhaps in part because of this, there has been a considerable expansion of the private healthcare sector in South Africa since the early 1990s, with much of the white population using their greater wealth to purchase private medical insurance and so guaranteeing their access to higher-quality services. Not only has this ensured that an income barrier has replaced a 'race' barrier in recent years, it has also presented a considerable challenge to the government in terms of human resources management. Lured by the better pay on offer in the private sector, much of the specialist medical labour is deployed in the private sector, despite the fact that it caters for a minority of the population. Indeed, in 1999, more than three quarters of the country's doctors and more than half of its professional nurses were employed in the private sector despite the fact that it catered for only around 20% of the population.

Added to this, the global nature of the medical sector has presented some tricky problems for the South African government. In particular, it has been hit hard by a 'brain drain', with thousands of doctors migrating to high-income countries. In part this has also been a consequence of efforts to expand access to healthcare. Much of the policy emphasis has been on creating clinics delivering basic care in previously underserved communities. While this strategy is an essential part of improving healthcare outcomes, the routine nature of much of the work performed in these clinics often does not appeal to highly skilled clinicians keen to develop careers based on medical specialisms. Not only have there been problems in staffing these clinics, but the emphasis on expanding basic care at the expense of specialist care has been cited by some as a contributory factor in the rising number of doctors migrating.

The global market has also played a significant role in holding back the South African government's plans for improving access to key treatments. In particular, the country faces real challenges as a consequence of the very high prevalence of HIV/AIDS, with more than five million people – more than 1 in 10 of the population – estimated to be living with HIV/AIDS. For many years, the government did not make life-extending anti-retroviral (ARV) drugs available, in part because some key political figures felt that alternative treatments might be more effective, but also because of doubts within the government about the cost-effectiveness of ARVs. With multinational drug companies pricing treatments as high as US$10,000 per person per year at the start of the millennium, the potential scale of the bill for providing ARVs seemed prohibitive and, moreover, laws protecting the intellectual property of the companies that had developed ARVs prevented cheap unbranded versions of the drugs (so-called 'generic' drugs) being produced locally. However, following much international lobbying, deals allowing the manufacture of cheap generics were agreed in 2002 and, with prices reduced to around US$100 per treatment per year, the South African government finally instituted a programme for distributing ARVs in 2004 (albeit later than some neighbours, a factor that brought not inconsiderable criticism). Unfortunately, while access to ARVs has been significantly extended, it is still far from universal and it is estimated that only one third of those needing ARVs received them in 2006 because, despite significant injections of funds estimated to be in excess of US$400 million per annum, programmes have lacked the resources needed to meet demand.

In most countries, the private sector plays at least some role in terms of the direct delivery of frontline health services. Again this role can take many different forms and varies widely in terms of scope. *Privately owned* for-profit and not-for-profit hospitals and health centres are widespread in most countries and in some are the dominant form of provision. While in some countries such private facilities can only be accessed by those with private funds (that is, those with private health insurance or sufficient cash to cover one-off payments), in others the state allows citizens to receive publicly funded treatments in private healthcare facilities. In Australia, for example, the public Medicare scheme can often be used to cover private doctors' fees so that the patient has a choice of treatment centres.

Added to this issue of the ownership of key healthcare facilities are often complicated issues about the *contractual status of key healthcare professionals*, particularly doctors (see Box 5.3). While in some countries the majority of doctors are private practitioners, in others the reverse is true and in many others doctors often share their time between public and (the often more lucrative) private practice. While this may seem something of a fine-grained issue, it can prove hugely important in policy terms, not least because the degree to which clinicians are under the employ of the state can have a major bearing on the degree to which the state can influence the activity of clinicians. If doctors' main source of income is government financed, then the political leverage of the state is usually increased.

Box 5.3	Paying doctors

Like education (see Chapter Four), a major feature of healthcare services is that they are *labour intensive*. Much of the healthcare budget consists of payments towards the salary costs of medical professionals and in most countries the healthcare workforce forms one of the largest occupational groups in every community. Yet, while all countries require the services of doctors in order to meet the healthcare needs of their citizens, how they procure these services varies significantly. This is particularly true with regard to primary care doctors (often referred to as general practitioners or family doctors) who often work alone or in small groups in small-scale local practices or clinics.

Perhaps the most straightforward mechanism is for general practitioners to be employed directly by the state as *salaried public sector employees*. In such cases, national pay rates are usually negotiated by professional associations, with some variations at the margins allowed to account for increased levels of expertise, specialisation or workload. While such an approach gives the government much certainty in terms of planning its annual labour costs and is easy to organise in administrative terms, fixed national salary levels can sometimes make it difficult to attract general practitioners to work in areas with higher living costs or more challenging workloads. Similarly, fixed national salaries may create disincentives for doctors to take on additional work or to adopt innovative techniques if they are not rewarded for doing so.

At the other extreme are schemes that pay doctors on a *fee-for-service* basis. Here, the government agree rates it is willing to pay for specific treatments and doctors are paid on the basis of the procedures they actually perform. This has the advantage of only paying doctors for the work they do and, in crude terms, of rewarding most heavily those who do the most work. It can also give doctors some freedom in terms of deciding how they want to balance their workload and reward those who respond best to patient demand. However, there are considerable disadvantages, including difficulties for the government in planning annual budgets in advance and the danger that doctors will be incentivised to prescribe more than is necessary or to offer treatments with higher rates even when there are reasonable alternatives that carry lower rates.

Finally, there is the option of using a *capitation payment system* in which doctors are simply paid a fixed amount for each patient registered with their practice. This approach offers something of a balance between the other two, rewarding more popular or heavily worked practices with higher payments, but without creating incentives to increase treatment levels or utilise the most expensive procedures. Nevertheless, there are risks that doctors may take on more patients than they can reasonably manage in such systems. In addition, if payments do not reflect the increased workload that might be attached to some patient groups (for example, older people) there may be a risk that doctors will have incentives to push such patients towards alternative providers.

As each of these approaches carries advantages and disadvantages, some countries try to combine two or three of them, by offering a basic salary that is topped up by fee-for-service or capitation payments, for instance.

Whether healthcare organisations are publicly or privately owned, the state always plays an important regulatory role. For example, the state is usually responsible for determining which drugs are deemed safe to go to market; which treatments (and at what cost) it will fund from public sources; who can legally practice as a doctor and what qualifications they need; and, in more general terms, the legal basis on which competition between private suppliers can take place. The state might also lay down guidelines regarding what standard of treatment individual patients can expect to receive, which treatments are deemed the most effective and, indeed, which suppliers it deems the most trustworthy or of the highest quality. It is in large part through these regulatory activities that the state aims to influence the quality of healthcare provision.

While we have focused the main part of our discussion here on clinical services, we should keep in mind the point we made right at the start of this chapter, that health policy stretches far beyond these boundaries. In particular, public health measures that are designed to prevent the spread of specific illnesses or diseases are vital, be they, for example, vaccination programmes, the banning of harmful drugs, policies for cutting the levels of damaging pollutants or, more generally still, workplace-based health and safety procedures. Added to this, the state can also play an important role in encouraging people to lead more healthy lives. Health promotion programmes aimed at, for instance, persuading people to smoke less, to eat more fruit and vegetables, to practise safe sex or to exercise regularly have an important role to play in boosting the health of nations. However, public health and health promotion activities usually draw more modest financial support from governments than medically based treatments: in high-income countries they typically account for little more than around 3% of total healthcare expenditure (OECD, 2007c).

Key policy issues

Earlier in this chapter we noted that healthcare provision is a subject of intense political debate in all countries. This is in no small part a consequence of the difficult balancing act governments face in reconciling the very large demand for healthcare services with the need to place some limits on the very large costs of healthcare. With public spending budgets increasingly squeezed in recent decades, the issues of **cost containment**, **value for money** and **service efficiency** have unsurprisingly risen up the health policy agenda. Although the strategies deployed by governments have varied, commonly exercised approaches have included:

- *tighter regulation and control* of medical practice, particularly in terms of recommending which treatments offer the best value for money;
- a related trend of *stronger management* of healthcare services (and, typically, an attempt to reduce the power of healthcare professionals to determine patterns of service provision in order to facilitate this);
- *increased one-off payments* from public service users (sometimes dubbed 'co-payments');
- *increased incentives* – usually in terms of tax breaks – for citizens to join private health insurance schemes in order to 'ease pressure' from public services; and
- injecting *greater competition* into public health services – by allowing public funds to be used to pay for private services and/or encouraging public hospitals or health centres to compete with each other – in the hope that competition for patients will drive down costs.

We should stress that these cost-containment measures have not always been about reducing costs per se: indeed, many countries have continued to see their health budgets rise. Yet many governments have undoubtedly tried to place a tighter grip on healthcare expenditure.

While guaranteeing value for money makes sense, the kinds of cost-containment strategies noted above do not come without consequences. Most notably, perhaps, attempts to increase the private part of the public–private mix of healthcare provision often increase the inequality of access to healthcare. As noted in the previous section, the major incentive for joining a private health insurance scheme is usually that it offers service on more favourable terms: quicker treatment or access to the newest clinical procedures, for instance. Yet because the costs of insurance are often out of reach for many people – either because their incomes are too low or because their poor healthcare status results in large premiums being quoted to them – greater use of private financing mechanisms will almost inevitably give some better healthcare services than others. Worse still, perhaps, the market failures we referred to earlier are likely to persist too, for the most favourable terms are likely to be offered to those least likely to be ill and vice versa for the simple reason that insurers have strong incentives to attract customers that are likely to return a profit (a process economists sometimes dub **cream skimming**). While such differences in access to goods and services may be tolerable with regard to luxury goods such as sports cars or flat-screen televisions, much deeper *moral questions* are invoked when access to the service in question is part of our basic human rights. These questions are particularly acute in low-income countries where public provision is patchy and where, consequently, access to modest services for some is contrasted with a much higher level of service provision for richer citizens able to cover the costs of private care (see Box 5.2).

Yet, these hugely important concerns about equity of access and the fulfilment of human rights need to be balanced against the rights of citizens to spend their own money as they so wish. Indeed, just as there is a strong moral case for limiting inequalities in access to healthcare, if the state feels the need to limit healthcare provision – and rationing at some point is an inevitability – then there is also a strong moral claim for allowing citizens to use their own money to fund, say, potentially life-saving surgery that the government believes is too experimental to justify the use of public funds. Indeed, few governments now place such restrictions on their citizens. In high-income countries with well-established and extensive public health services, these tensions between containing the costs of public services on the one hand and trying to limit the inequities that arise from widespread use of private alternatives by the better-off on the other have arguably been exacerbated in recent years by rising expectations of consumers and the ever-increasing scope of medical care as a consequence of technological and scientific advancement. In many of these countries, debate about the quality of services has intensified and, with governments unable to meet the full extent of demand for healthcare services, even nations with the best-funded services have witnessed an increase in the size of their private healthcare markets since the start of the 1980s. In Sweden, for instance, private healthcare expenditure accounted for just 7% of total healthcare spending in 1980, but by 2005 it had more than doubled to 15.4% of total health spending (OECD, 2007c).

In part, then, rising private expenditures are a response to the *dilemmas of healthcare rationing*. We noted earlier that all healthcare systems must exercise some form of rationing. The traditional response in social democratic systems has been to ration via waiting lists: when capacity is limited, patients will be added to a queue based on the urgency of their case and asked to wait (sometimes for many months) for their turn. Added to this, rationing has also increasingly taken place on the basis of publicly determined judgements about the effectiveness or value for money provided by specific interventions. In short, public systems need public gatekeepers – sometime doctors, sometimes bureaucrats – who will restrict access to services. By contrast, private systems do not restrict access on the basis of such rules. Instead, rationing is determined by the market conditions. If capacity is scarce then the price goes up and those who cannot afford treatment will miss out. It is important to note, therefore, that rising private expenditures do not resolve issues surrounding healthcare rationing, but merely allow some people to circumvent the queues or closed gates presented to them by public systems. Moreover, in predominantly private systems such as the US, we often find considerable numbers of people who have to go without healthcare because they are priced out of the market: more than 45 million US citizens had no insurance in 2005 for instance (OECD, 2007c).

That said, we should again be wary of painting a one-sided picture here. While private expenditure has risen in many countries since the 1980s, in some countries there is an intensive debate about how to extend the scale and scope of public provision. In the first few years of the new millennium, for example, Liberia, Malawi and Rwanda all witnessed considerable increases – between 20 and 30 percentage points – in the share of health spending accounted for by public funds following considerable injections of additional finance (UNDP, 2007). But this is not just the case in the low-income countries. Interestingly, some of the high-income countries noted for their relatively weak welfare states have increased their healthcare spending considerably in recent years. In the UK, for instance, one of the legacies of the Blair governments was a considerable increase in the share of national income devoted to public expenditure on healthcare; indeed, private spending actually fell as a percentage of total healthcare during Blair's time in office.

However, reform in the healthcare sector can often be slow moving, not least because the will of governments can be counteracted by very strong external interests. We noted at the start of the chapter that healthcare is big business in many countries. One consequence of this is that big businesses are usually keen to protect their business interests. Very large multinational pharmaceutical and medical supplies companies, for instance, work hard to ensure that their intellectual property rights are respected and their profit margins protected. Governments in many countries have become concerned about the rising costs of prescription medicines, but can find it tough to drive costs down because patent protections often restrict production of a drug – particularly a new one – to the company that developed it. Similarly, private health insurance companies usually lobby to resist expansion of state activity in healthcare for fear it will encroach on their own business.

In all the fields of policy we consider in this book there are many competing interests that continually use their influence to shape policy, but many political scientists have highlighted healthcare as a special case because of the relative *political strength of the medical profession* and the difficulties this can create for governments looking to push through reforms that challenge the interests of the profession (Hudson, and Lowe,

2004). This strength is evident both at the collective and the individual level and both dimensions are worth briefly considering.

At the individual level, managers often find it very difficult to impose policy on individual clinicians. In large part this is because the sheer complexity of many medical interventions makes it very difficult for non-medical specialists to observe, measure and understand the nuances of medical practice. Many attempts to increase the accountability of clinicians to managers by, for instance, using detailed computer-based accounting packages to track their work activity, have struggled because such computer systems rely heavily on the medics themselves to provide information about their own work patterns; if doctors are unwilling to cooperate with the collection of data then the systems are of limited use. Moreover, even if they are willing to cooperate, the collection of data can be a very time-consuming and costly exercise that diverts resources away from patient care. This is a problem that affects both public and private suppliers of healthcare. Indeed, if anything, it is a greater issue for private providers for they need much more detailed data on activity in order to bill insurers and, equally, private insurers demand more detailed data in order to be sure they are not being overcharged; this is reflected in the much higher administrative costs in private and more market-based public systems. For example, in Chile these costs soared after privatisation of the healthcare system. Interestingly, many of the cost-containment measures introduced in recent decades have led to an increase in the number of managers in health systems and in overall administrative costs. While better management certainly holds the potential to deliver better value for money and, indeed, more efficient delivery of healthcare services, in some countries a backlash against this trend has resulted in attempts to reduce the number of managers in order to free up resources for frontline services.

At the collective level, medics are usually strongly represented by powerful professional associations that are well respected and well connected within government circles. In many countries, these organisations are consulted by the government as a matter of course when healthcare reforms are being considered and, consequently, are well placed to make the interests of the profession heard. While it certainly makes sense to consult the medical profession before making any radical changes to healthcare services, some have argued that the interests of the profession are heard too strongly and that health services too often serve the medical profession's interests at the expense of patient interests. It is certainly the case that medics are usually very well paid and are often offered favourable terms of public practice that, for instance, allow them time to undertake private duties in addition to their publicly funded roles.

More generally, however, some sociologists have argued that health services might be better termed **sickness services**. This critique suggests that, in part because of the power of the medical profession, health policy is dominated by the so-called **biomedical model** of health. This model of healthcare emphasises clinical interventions that address illness and disease and can be contrasted with a **social model** of health that emphasises the importance of broader environmental factors in shaping healthcare outcomes. Indeed, one of the major ironies of health policy is that once reasonable service levels have been established for all, it becomes difficult to establish a link between increased levels of expenditure on medical services and improved healthcare outcomes such as life expectancy or infant mortality. Indeed, despite having the highest level of healthcare spending in the world, the US actually has a lower level of life expectancy than virtually every Western European country (see Figure 5.1). Some have even argued that the biggest health outcome gains have resulted from public health measures that do not rely on medical intervention: removing impurities from water supplies, improved levels of nutrition or making the use of seatbelts in cars compulsory, for instance (McKeown, 1979). Yet funding for these measures is minimal compared with funding for medical interventions, perhaps in part because the political emphasis is firmly on the biomedical model in most countries.

Although we should be very wary of denigrating the huge value of effective medical interventions, the importance of a broader social understanding of healthcare becomes clear when we consider health inequalities within nations. In many countries there are often stark contrasts in, for instance, the life expectancy of people with different income levels: in the UK in

Figure 5.1: Health spending and outcomes, 2004

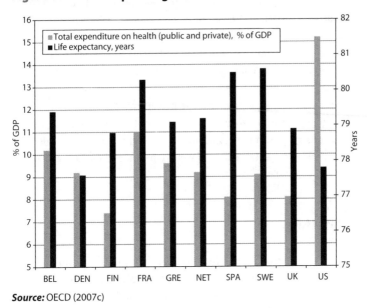

Source: OECD (2007c)

the mid-1990s, the life expectancy of someone from the unskilled or partially skilled occupational class was more than five years shorter than that for someone from the professional and managerial occupational class. Moreover, because income inequalities often interact with other social divisions, there are sometimes even starker differences between different groups of people. In Australia, for instance, at the start of the new millennium, an Aboriginal or Torres Straits Islander male had a life expectancy of just 59 years, almost two decades shorter than the 77 years a non-indigenous male could expect. These major differences in life chances are fundamentally shaped by broad social inequalities in societies – particularly the quality of living and working environments – and cannot be mitigated by medical services alone. Moreover, in some nations these inequalities are reinforced by the healthcare system itself. In the US, for example, in 2005 11.3% of non-Hispanic white people did not have health insurance coverage, compared with 19.6% of black people and 32.7% of Hispanic people.

What this points to is that healthcare outcomes, healthcare systems and broader social and environmental factors are heavily interlinked. Indeed, the so-called **biopsychosocial model of health** recognises that our physical, mental and social well-being are heavily related and promotes a much broader perspective of healthcare. Although we have focused primarily on medical services here to constrain the scope of our chapter, it is important that the broad links between health policy and other key pillars such as housing, social security and social care are not forgotten. In fact, some would argue that joining up healthcare services with other key pillars of welfare is one of the major challenges facing policy makers.

SUMMARY

- ■ Healthcare is one of the **largest items of public spending**.
- ■ Healthcare systems almost always involve a complex **mixed economy** of public and private provision and funding.
- ■ All health services **ration** the supply of healthcare in order to cope with the pressures of **demand**.
- ■ Levels of demand for health services are **rising** not least because of **technological and demographic change**.
- ■ Most countries' health policies have shown a greater concern with **cost-containment** measures in recent years.
- ■ All healthcare systems have some **inequalities of access** and the structure of those systems can contribute to inequalities.
- ■ Healthcare outcomes are fundamentally shaped by **underlying social and economic inequalities**.
- ■ Governments face unusually **strong political interests** in the arena of health policy and this can present difficulties for policy making and for the management of health services.

READING GUIDE

An excellent and longstanding introductory text is Ham's (2004) *Health policy in Britain* and Baggott's (2007) *Understanding health policy* is also very useful. Both texts focus mainly on the British case, however; a more international perspective is provided by Blank and Burau (2007). Nettleton's (2006) *The sociology of health and illness* provides a very good overview of the medical sociology literature. Glennerster (2003) offers an accessible guide to issues surrounding the financing of healthcare. Smith (2003) provides an extensive discussion of healthcare inequalities.

The OECD provides much easily accessible information about healthcare systems and healthcare spending on its website (www.oecd.org). Its *OECD health data* (2007c) package is particularly useful and provides data on a wide range of healthcare-related activities. The UNDP (www.undp.org/) provides data on a smaller range of indicators but for a much larger set of countries as part of its *Human development report* series (UNDP, 2007) and the World Health Organization (www.who.int) also provides much data via its website, including access to WHOSIS – the World Health Organization Statistical Information System (WHO, 2007).

6

housing

Introduction

In terms of people's welfare and well-being, having a roof over their heads – housing – is hard to beat in terms of significance. Article 25 of the *Universal Declaration of Human Rights* (UN Assembly, 1948) lists housing as being an essential right necessary for people's health and well-being and Article 12 notes that the home is a private sanctuary in which citizens must be free from undue interference of their privacy. The home is the central focus of most people's lives and is typically the focal point of family life.

Housing policy is naturally, therefore, a major concern of governments. However, it is often suggested that housing differs from the other pillars of welfare examined in this book because such a high proportion of it is supplied and distributed through the private sector. Indeed, in most countries it is common to talk of the **housing market** rather than a housing service, because it is not unusual for between 60% and 80% of housing to be supplied through the **private market** either as rental properties managed by private landlords or as privately owned homes that are bought and sold by individual citizens. Even in societies with a high proportion of state-owned housing or where the state attempts to oversee the private rental part of the housing market (such as in Germany and Sweden), home ownership and private landlords together make up the majority of housing provision. In addition, the vast majority of housing – whether state or market – is *built* by private construction companies.

Housing also differs from key areas of the welfare state in so far as a high proportion of the resources expended in the area comes in the form of capital expenditure on 'bricks and mortar' and the purchase of building land. Many other pillars of welfare – education, healthcare and employment training, for example – are primarily *services* delivered to people and are very labour intensive rather than capital intensive or, in the case of social security, are focused on recurrent cash transfers rather than long-term investments.

In other chapters we have tried to give an indication of the scale of the size of each pillar by referring to the overall level of government spending in the sector; as will become clear during the course of this chapter, it is difficult to provide equivalent figures for housing because spending is haphazard and spread across many different functions and, moreover, because government policy often aims to influence activity in the private sphere without directly controlling it. Indeed, housing has been described as 'the *wobbly pillar* under the welfare state' because of these features and much of the welfare state literature mistakenly downplays housing because of its reliance on the open market. It is important at the outset to realise that, despite this, housing is still a major pillar with which the state is closely concerned.

It also important to note that the very concept of 'the home' has what are often very deep cultural roots in each nation – the very words 'home' and 'housing' conjure up mental images that delve deeply into our psyche (see Box 6.1). Yet those images may vary vastly from nation to nation, be it in terms of the style of the typical home, its size, the standard of amenities that might be expected within the home, the number of people who typically occupy the household or who is likely to own the property. Furthermore, while the home is a place of security and belonging for many, housing is often vulnerable and the home can be a vulnerable place. **Homelessness** is a major social problem in many countries and results in people being separated from the normal securities and comforts of a home (Lowe, 2004).

| **Box 6.1** | **The concept of 'home'** |

The idea of 'home' is universally and instinctively understood. People who have lived abroad talk about 'coming home'. We intuitively think of home in relation to the wider world 'out there' beyond our front doors. The concept is closely bound up with creating our own self-identity – where we are most 'ourselves'. The sociologist Giddens (1991) suggests that the home is the main place where social life is sustained and above all reproduced. The French sociologist Bachelard (1992) believed that the home was critical to our deepest psychic well-being and that rooms, pieces of furniture, nooks and crannies in the house – how they smell, their echoes and their secret memories – makes the home a sanctuary; as he says, 'the house allows one to dream in peace' (Bachelard, 1992, p 4).

A good example of the idea of home in practice is the idea of domesticity, which was invented in 19th-century England. Victorian domestic culture was imbued with a sense of the home as a retreat from a hostile world outside. This powerful culture with its strong moral purpose spread across the British Empire and took root in all the English-speaking nations. Throughout the 20th century, interest in the domestic interior persisted and found expression in the obsession with home decoration and the 'make-over' of rooms and gardens, as seen in numerous television programmes. This sense of being acceptably fashionable is not a new idea and is a contemporary expression of conformity through home-making.

In the 21st century, the digital revolution and the invention of the internet has transformed how people's homes are used, with a huge increase in 'home-working', new types of leisure activity (for example, home-cinema) and new relationships with commercial organisations (for example, home-banking). In an era of globalisation when we all reside on a planet where time and space have new meanings, it is clear that the home is ever more important to people's social and psychological well-being. Home has always been the focal point of human life and this is as true in the 21st century as it was for our cave-dwelling ancestors.

Key policy goals

As our introduction should make clear, while housing is a very personal and, in many ways, private issue, housing is also of great concern to the state in terms of a number of fundamental policy issues.

Chief among the concerns of the government is the need to ensure that there is an *adequate supply of housing*. Changing population levels, increasing life expectancy, changing family formations, migration, the movement of people in and out of different regions of a nation or even in and out of different parts of a town or city all create challenges in terms of the housing supply. A vital part of housing policy is to try to match the quantity of homes in any given area with the number that need to be supplied in relation to the current and forecast number of households.

Added to this, changing lifestyles and family forms require the government not only to plan supply on the basis of the number of homes needed, but to also think about the *type and size of properties* that are needed to meet the needs of modern family types. Fluctuating birthrates, life expectancy, marriage rates and divorce rates can all influence the demand for different sizes and types of property and, again, there is a need to manage supply to account for this. Similarly, changing economic fortunes or consumer expectations, even changing fashions, have a role to play in influencing the level of demand for different types of housing (Bramley et al, 2004).

Closely linked to the issue of the size and type of properties are issues surrounding the *standard of housing*. As noted in other chapters, the quality of housing fundamentally influences healthcare outcomes and well-being more generally. In addition, living in poor-quality housing is often an outcome of income-related poverty and can contribute towards social exclusion. Improving the standard of housing, therefore, can be important not only as a goal of housing policy, but also in addressing broader social policy issues.

Finally, and on a related note, the *affordability of housing* is a crucial issue. High housing costs can create major social problems, be it in terms of contributing to income poverty by stretching household budgets to their limits, reducing the flexibility of employment markets by presenting barriers to the movement of labour across a country, limiting family formation by restricting the size of families beyond that desired or, more simply, preventing people from leading a happy life because of the stresses of locating housing near to friends and family.

How governments meet these policy goals, however, varies somewhat from country to country. We will deal with the key policy mechanisms in more detail in the next section, but in general terms it is possible to divide most high-income nations into one of two broad housing systems.

First, there are *home-owning dominated* societies in which the majority of houses are private properties owned by individual citizens. In such systems the housing market often acts as a major driver of the economy, with housing being a major focus of personal investment, and a key role of the state is to ensure the smooth running of the market and, frequently, to stimulate its growth. However, the costs of purchasing houses are such that not everyone will be able to afford to own their own home or, indeed, want to, so a significant proportion of the population will still rent homes. In such systems there is typically a clear separation between public and private renting. Private renting is usually unsubsidised and fully commercial in pricing, effectively an adjunct of the home ownership market, with private property owners free to buy, sell or rent their properties with relatively few restrictions. Public renting, meanwhile, is typically a residual state-run safety net for low-income households with rents usually subsidised by the state. On top of this, the state often supports those on low incomes via indirect subsidies of private renting in the form of housing allowances paid through the social security system (see Chapter Two). This type of housing system is typical of the high-income English-speaking nations such as the UK, the US and Australia (Kemeny, 1981).

The second type of housing system that many countries operate, by contrast, is the *mixed/plural system* in which there is a more balanced approach. Here, owner-occupation remains an important part of the overall picture, but is not such a driving force and there is less pressure on those who can afford to do so to buy their own home. Instead, both public and private renting play larger roles and although the two sectors are again clearly separated they usually operate in the context of a more harmonised rent-setting system that is overseen by the state. Indeed, this regulation of rents is one of the factors that gives renting a broader appeal in these countries. In other words, the market is more heavily constrained in these systems and the state's role extends beyond that of provider of residual housing as a supplement to a favoured private market. This system is commonly found in Northern and Western Europe.

A third possibility is a *state-led housing* system in which the government takes the lead role in building, allocating and maintaining housing. Here, the role of the private market is heavily constrained and, sometimes, in principle, eliminated. Typically, in these systems a restricted form of home ownership in which private individuals can own the property they live in but cannot sell their home to others accompanies the option of renting from the public sector. What this means in practice is that the state allocates and reallocates property – both rented and privately owned – and so the market mechanism is replaced with a bureaucratic approach (Lowe and Tsenkova, 2003). This also means that there is little in the way of commercial construction (indeed, sometimes it is banned in such systems), with house building largely undertaken by the state or in the form of families self-building their own home. Such an approach is rare following the collapse of the Communist bloc in Eastern and Central Europe (see Box 6.2), and not found in high-income countries at all, but still broadly characterises the housing system in Cuba, for instance.

In each of these systems of housing the state plays an important role, but it differs widely from that of market regulator and provider of last-resort safety net through to main provider. Likewise, the role of the private market also varies, from dominant provider, through restricted provider to minority player. Significantly, these differing roles for the state and the market usually reflect differing values and goals with regard to the role of the housing market in generating wealth. While in home-owning dominated systems the market is left to operate relatively freely because it is viewed as an important source of *wealth and asset accumulation*, in other systems stronger restrictions are placed on the market in order to emphasise *broader social concerns* surrounding housing affordability. Indeed, in state-led housing systems it is typically illegal to profit from property development and property speculation, while in the more free-market home-owning systems the state often encourages consumers to store their wealth in property and to profit from property development.

Box 6.2	Post-Communist housing

One of the most dramatic political changes in recent years was the collapse of the USSR and the other European Communist states. Under the Communist system a large share of housing production was organised and managed by the state. There were, however, considerable variations to the balance of state and private housing. For example in Hungary nearly 80% of new housing between 1946 and 1990 was self-built (private building firms were not allowed) – people used their own resources and labour. Housing was used as an incentive to ensure that key workers – doctors, teachers, engineers and so on – moved to where they were needed. Generally, the state provided housing at very low costs and cheap food but in a very low-wage economy. In fact, housing was traded on a massive scale through a black market of cash and 'hard currency' deals. Most rural housing in all these countries was and remained owner-occupied.

When Communism collapsed at the end of the 1980s, most of the economies were bankrupt and state flats were sold simply because local governments could not afford to manage and maintain them. Selling state flats at low prices was also a 'shock absorber' for the dramatic changes to these economies that were taking place as they adjusted to global market prices. Because private renting had been virtually abolished under Communism and because most state rental flats were sold, these countries have become 'super-owner-occupied'. Countries such as Hungary, Romania and Bulgaria have home-owning rates in excess of 90% of households. Other nations have retained some of their rental stock but mostly the emphasis has been on rapid privatisation.

China's economy has also been liberalised since 1978 although the country remains a socialist state. A policy for the gradual privatisation of housing has also been followed, in parallel with the European post-Communist nations. State flats have been progressively sold off and an open property market is developing rapidly alongside the marketisation of the wider Chinese economy.

Home ownership has come to dominate many post-Communist societies, producing a completely new variety of housing system, and it remains to be seen what the wider impact on society and the emerging welfare states will be.

Key delivery mechanisms

As we have already made clear, all housing systems involve some mix of public and privately owned properties and, in addition, a distinction can be drawn between those who own their own home (**owner-occupiers**) and those who rent their home. Owning and renting are the two principal forms of **housing tenure**. The idea of 'tenure' arises because housing is lived in (consumed) by private individual households behind their own front doors. This is a key difference between housing and other welfare pillars such as health and education because they are mainly services provided in a collective setting – a hospital ward, a school classroom and so on. The word tenure comes from the Latin verb *teneo, tenire*, which means 'to hold' and tenure indicates who has possession of a property.

Owner-occupiers either own their home (and the land on which it is built) outright or are in the process of buying it using a special form of loan called a mortgage. Strong property rights are a feature of most democracies and, as a consequence, home owners have considerable autonomy in the running of their homes and it is difficult to remove someone's right to occupy the property as a consequence. This provides considerable security for home owners but also creates rigidity in the housing market. Property ownership can also provide individuals with a valuable asset that acts as an important form of wealth accumulation. Set against this, owner-occupiers are responsible for the upkeep of their property and can be exposed to considerable financial risk as a consequence. Similarly, if an owner-occupier is in the process of paying a mortgage on a property, then failure to meet repayments on that loan can lead to them losing their property to the lender.

Those who rent their rooms, flat or house from a landlord who owns the property are known as **tenants**. Landlords come in many forms and can be the state, a private individual, a company or a non-governmental organisation. For tenants, payment of a weekly rent to the landlord gives the tenant legal occupation of the dwelling in a package of rights and responsibilities. The advantage of renting over ownership is that tenants do not have to worry about the basic maintenance of the property and it is much easier and cheaper to move on elsewhere should the property be no longer suitable.

A third, but much less common, form of tenure in some countries is **leaseholder**. This form of tenure usually exists when one large building is split into multiple properties: a block of flats, for example. In such instances, a distinction can be drawn between the freeholder – who owns the building as a whole in perpetuity – and the individual leaseholders who buy long-term leases (99 years is common) that give them ownership of, say, one of the flats in the apartment block. Typically, the leaseholder has responsibility for the upkeep of the internal aspects of their property, while the freeholder is responsible for communal areas (for example, stairways, corridors) and the fabric of the building itself.

Although there is a specific legal package of rights and responsibilities associated with each of the principal tenures they are not in strict law always as different from each other as might be imagined. In some countries, tenancy rights are so secure that they amount to control over the property normally associated with ownership. For example, the tenancy can be inherited by family members. In most legal systems around the world a tenancy agreement means that the owner of the property (the landlord) gives up their right of possession for the period of the tenancy, although many private landlords often imagine that it is still 'theirs' and find it hard to accept that the house or flat is out of their control.

Irrespective of the tenure of a property, the physical manifestation of housing provides a distinctive feature of this pillar of welfare. Much of the expenditure in the housing field comes during the construction of a property and, once it is built, it cannot be moved. All of these factors mean that considerable effort needs to go into the management and maintenance of the existing housing stock. Indeed, housing needs to be thought of as a process rather than a one-off construction event, and there are four main stages in the 'housing process': development, construction, allocation and repair and maintenance. We will briefly consider each in turn.

Property **development** involves someone initiating a scheme to build, be it commercial builders, government organisations, private individuals or non-governmental organisations. At this stage, suitable land must be located for the development and the land bought. In many countries the state sometimes looks to stimulate development in specific geographic areas – perhaps because there is an undersupply of housing there or it wants to regenerate the area – and so offers financial incentives such as tax breaks or subsidies to those prepared to undertake development. Normally, planning permission needs to be gained from government-appointed planning authorities whose role is to monitor the environment and to ensure that the development addresses government house-building targets in the area. The planning authorities may also restrict developments they feel are not in keeping with an area or are in conflict with broader government policy objectives. This stage is followed by a **construction** phase, with private contractors – typically either small speculative builders or large building companies – being commissioned to undertake the work, even if the developer is the state itself (Bramley et al, 2004).

Once construction is complete, the process of **allocation** needs to occur. At this stage, the housing process changes from being about production to 'consumption'. Normally, the legal title for both the property and the land changes to a new owner, who might be an owner-occupier or a landlord (either a speculative private landlord or a social housing body), and a price for the sale is agreed. A further stage may involve a procedure for selecting a tenant. Later on the property is likely to be resold or reallocated.

Finally, there is a crucial phase of **repair and maintenance**. As the property ages so it will require routine maintenance to preserve its life expectancy. One of the main functions of the state in relation to housing is to ensure that housing standards are maintained, both when properties are built (typically structural plans have to be approved to demonstrate that they meet modern standards) and as time goes by such that they remain in a condition fit for habitation. Governments in high-income countries usually monitor housing conditions in regular surveys of the housing stock. This sometimes leads to renewal and renovation strategies and when necessary clearance of unfit property. Almost always 'slum clearance' is a state activity managed by local governments. Often properties earmarked for demolition are owned by private landlords and the demolition programme involves replacing them with new state housing – housing that is owned and managed by local authorities, federal governments or state-financed housing associations/cooperatives.

The relatively fixed nature of housing – particularly when privately owned – needs to be stressed here. It is the existence of historical housing that marks housing as a little different from the other welfare state pillars. Housing is fixed and durable and the stock is added to very slowly; typically less than 1% of new housing is added per annum. As a result, housing is usually (although not always) much slower to change than the other areas of social policy and many housing problems arise from this historical legacy.

Running in parallel to these four stages is the crucial issue of *housing finance*. Housing production is very expensive compared to average household income. As a result, governments often have to have regard not only to whether a sufficient quantity of housing is being built but also that the 'consumers' (owners and tenants alike) can afford to pay the often high costs of housing.

As noted above, most owner-occupiers have bought or are in the process of buying their home. Because the cost of a house or flat can typically be anything between three and ten times the size of annual household incomes, some mechanism is needed to spread out the costs over a long period of time. This is done in the form of long loans called mortgages in which credit is paid back over a period usually ranging from 15 to 30 years but with a large amount of interest on the outstanding debt. Here, in broad terms, the property and the loan are tied together, with the lender (usually a bank or a building society) retaining the title deeds that assign legal ownership of the property until the full extent of the loan is paid off. Crucially, the terms of the contract signed when a mortgage is arranged allow for the lender to repossess the property if the household cannot afford the repayments on the loan. This entails the lender retaking ownership of the property and then selling it in order to get their money back. Obviously repossession is an extremely stressful event and, in some countries, governments offer financial support to owner-occupiers who risk losing their home as a consequence of a change in their financial status: in Finland, for example, there is a relatively generous 'home loan guarantee' scheme.

If all goes well, an owner-occupier's home is not only a place to live but can also be a considerable financial asset. Most owner-occupiers have considerable equity in their house – the difference between the current market value of the house and what they owe any lender on a mortgage – and can borrow against this equity to release capital for other purposes. Often such borrowing funds private welfare consumption such as the payment of a child's school or university fees or the funding of one-off medical interventions. Similarly, for many home owners their house forms an important part of their overall investment plans for retirement, with many moving to smaller/cheaper houses later in life and using the surplus equity they release in so doing to supplement pensions or cover the costs of care (Lowe, 2004).

Owner-occupation may sometimes seem like a private matter that has little to do with the government, but this is not so. Even in countries in which home owning dominates, the state still plays a strong role in regulating housing standards and in controlling how properties can be modified through planning laws. In addition, some countries provide tax subsidies to those purchasing property (for example, by allowing mortgage interest payments to be offset against income tax payments) or similar incentive schemes. Conversely, it is sometimes the case that when countries offer welfare services on a means-tested basis the value of property is taken into account as part of an asset test, meaning those with property of considerable value may be excluded from receiving state funding for particular services. More generally, the state also oversees the housing property market and plays a huge role in terms of promoting its stability and smooth running. In particular, its economic policies play a huge role in influencing the cost of mortgage repayments because in most countries the government either sets interest rates directly or has considerable influence over the independent central banks that do so.

Although tenants themselves do not have the long-term commitment of a mortgage, they still play an important role in the housing finance market because their rent goes to a landlord who has to pay a mortgage (or who makes a large profit if the debt has been paid off). One of the disadvantages of renting is that tenants never own the equity of the property – even if they have lived in it their entire adult life – and, indeed, the fruits of the investment they have largely funded go entirely to the landlord. Moreover, not only do tenants miss out on these capital gains, they also pay rent continuously for their whole life rather than paying towards a mortgage for a fixed period.

Given the often high costs of housing and the considerable wealth that can be tied to privately owned property, housing can fundamentally influence the distribution of wealth and income and heavily shape income poverty and income inequality. Consequently, most countries put in place mechanisms for addressing potential imbalances arising from this division in the housing market.

On the one hand, as we have noted above, governments in many countries subsidise rent levels, by: offering social housing to those on low incomes at sub-market rents; regulating the rents that can be charged by private landlords to ensure a broad degree of affordability or fairness; or by offering housing allowances to low-income households via the social security system. In terms of the latter, some countries offer dedicated payments (for example the UK has a specific 'housing benefit'), while others include such payments as part of regular unemployment benefit payments or pension payments for instance.

On the other hand, most governments also tax the capital gains accrued from privately owned property. Mechanisms for doing this include levying charges on profits when a landlord sells a property that was not their primary home and taxing income raised from property rents. In addition, most countries have some form of inheritance tax that places a charge on estates when a property owner dies; these taxes play an important role in rebalancing wealth within nations, for the transfer of property assets from one generation to the next heavily reinforces income differentials between social classes.

A more radical strategy to address divides between property owners and renters that some governments have adopted has been to allow those in rented public housing to buy their house from the state at a heavily discounted rate. These privatisations of public housing are usually part of a concerted policy effort to increase home ownership rates. In terms of easing the move towards home ownership, some countries have also implemented programmes that offer financial assistance (usually in the form of a subsidised loan) to key public sector workers for whom the cost of housing is out of reach and, similarly, some governments use planning laws to place pressure on developers to include some affordable housing in any major new property developments.

While many of these mechanisms aim to address questions of housing affordability, homelessness is an issue in all societies (see Box 6.3). The bottom line here is that in every society problems arise because there is not enough property at a price people can afford or simply because there is an insufficient supply (Burrows et al, 1997). Overcrowded houses, rough sleepers on the streets, housing in poor physical shape and excessively high house prices are all symptoms that there is something wrong in the balance of households to dwellings. It is the aim of most governments to try to promote sufficient supply of an adequate standard of housing. What is deemed an adequate standard depends very much on the wider economic health of particular nations. What is then done about implementing the standard varies considerably according to the policy direction taken by governments of different political persuasions. As a general rule, governments try to advance housing standards in line with economic growth.

Box 6.3   Homelessness

Homelessness is a more complex state than is commonly understood. The European Observatory on Homelessness (see Edgar and Meert, 2006) suggests a four-way definition that captures different types of homelessness well:

- **Rooflessness:** defined as being without any kind of shelter for all or most of the day. This includes people sleeping rough or having access only to a night shelter.
- **Houselessness:** defined as having a temporary place to stay in an institution or shelter. This includes people living in a hostel for the homeless, temporary accommodation for those

recently released from prison but with no other fixed address or a reception centre for recently arrived migrants.

- **Living in insecure housing:** defined as those with insecure tenancies or unsafe housing. This includes people renting properties without proper legal contracts to secure their tenancy, those staying temporarily with friends or family, people occupying housing from which they are soon to be evicted (for example, for non-payment of rent) and those whose housing is unsafe because of the threat of domestic violence.
- **Living in inadequate housing:** defined as those living in unfit or illegal housing. This includes people living in caravans that are not on legal sites, anyone living in makeshift housing, people living in extremely overcrowded housing and those in houses that fail to meet legal safety standards.

This classification not only usefully breaks homelessness down into a series of discrete but rather different subcategories, it also highlights well the link between homelessness and the concept of the home (see Box 6.1).

From an empirical viewpoint, the classification also allows for a more accurate measurement of the nature and extent of homelessness. For example, a recent report that used this classification noted that there were an estimated 5,080 rough sleepers in France, but that there were also 46,469 living in homelessness hostels, an estimated 150,000 living temporarily with family or friends, some 2,000 living in illegal buildings, 103,285 living under the threat of eviction, 1,150,000 living in unfit housing and 1,037,000 in overcrowded housing (Edgar and Meert, 2006).

How a particular nation responds to housing shortages also depends on circumstances that are often beyond its control. For example, almost all the nations of Western and Central Europe suffered dramatic setbacks in their housing programmes as a result of the First and Second World Wars during the 20th century, a combined total of over 10 years when almost no housing was built, there was considerable destruction of civilian property and demand from new households soared. In Britain, for example, the Second World War created a deficit of households to dwellings of nearly 2 million by 1945 in a housing stock of only 12.5 million (Holmans, 2000). It was this level of massive deficit that was the context for post-war housing policy in almost every European nation and was one of the contributory factors in the widespread deployment of easy-to-build, prefabricated, concrete, high-rise tower blocks.

Moreover, housing shortages do not arise solely as a consequence of dramatic shocks that damage housing stock such as war or earthquakes. Housing shortages typically arise because of more gradual changes in the population and lifestyle. Indeed, an important feature of the issue of the balance of households to dwellings is the fact that in high-income societies the number of households grows faster than the population due to improvements in life expectancy and incomes. Put simply, when the number of adults in the population increases this results in a larger pool of people potentially wanting to form a household. Added to this, other basic demographic changes can be significant. For example, in many countries there has been a rapid growth in the number of single-person households. In Europe this tendency began during the Second World War with an increase in the number of widows but is now primarily a product of increasing divorce rates and to a lesser extent a rise in the number of people who make a lifestyle choice to live alone. All these changes mean that there is an increasing number of households relative to the size of the population. Strategic planning on the basis of population forecasts is therefore an important component of housing policy.

Key policy issues

As is no doubt evident by now, housing is a complex field of social policy in which the state has to balance a wide range of public and private concerns. In so doing, it is faced with numerous policy dilemmas and the often slow-moving nature of housing change can make it difficult to rapidly reshape the nature of housing provision.

Indeed, the housing stock in any nation consists of all the accumulated dwellings built in the past, representing many different styles of building, designs and building programmes. Each nation's own specific history will have a profound impact on its housing stock. For example, as we have noted, in most European countries after the Second World War a high proportion of new housing was built in the form of high-rise blocks of flats that, quite literally, had a towering impact on the urban landscape that persists today in many places. In recent years some of the biggest of these have been blown up in some countries because they were regarded as undesirable and became associated with social problems. But, in other cities – such as Stockholm, Budapest and Vienna – high-rise flats have a long tradition and have not been viewed in a negative light. In the UK, the effects of its very early industrialisation and consequent urbanisation are still felt today in its housing stock: a very high proportion of the housing in its major cities is old, with more than a quarter being built in the 19th century despite subsequent slum clearance programmes and extensive bomb damage during the Blitz in the Second World War.

Balancing the rights of property owners with a need to modernise housing stock is a tricky issue, particularly if policy makers have plans for rapid modernisation of a specific area or if rapid social and economic change are producing intense pressures on housing in a particular area. Indeed, some of the most stunning examples of economic development in recent years come in nations where the state has restricted individual property rights in order to prioritise collective goals. In Singapore, for instance, the skyline has undergone dramatic transformation in recent decades with many old-style, brick-built, two-storey dwellings and commercial properties having been replaced with modern skyscrapers. However, this transformation was only possible because the government regularly used its powers to undertake compulsory purchase of private property in order to facilitate its redevelopment schemes. While some would say that the rapid economic growth delivered by the government justifies its approach – particularly given the shortage of land in what is a tiny city state – others feel that the human rights of individual property owners have been breached and that, sometimes, whole communities have been powerless to prevent redevelopments that have threatened their traditional focal points, meeting places and, indeed, way of life.

Yet, without change in the housing stock, economic development can certainly be constrained in a significant way and social problems can arise if there is insufficient property to meet demand in a specific location. As noted above, achieving an *appropriate balance of households to dwellings* is, therefore, always a challenge for policy makers. Delivering an appropriate balance, however, is a task that can be fraught with political difficulties. On top of the issues just discussed about the rights of individual property developers, housing expansion programmes may also need to grapple with sensitive environmental issues. If cities are crowded with properties, and the demand for housing expands, then questions about whether to extend the city limits into previously undeveloped or underdeveloped land can arise. Often this means building on rural greenfield sites and this can be hugely problematic. Indeed, there is a broader debate about environmentally **sustainable development** that is hugely important in this context, for a balance between different types of land usage is essential, yet housing needs often take precedence. In places with rapid economic growth and high population density these problems can be particularly acute. In Hong Kong, for instance, there have been some radical land reclamation schemes that have involved extending the boundaries of the city into the sea. While this has created much-needed additional space in one of the most crowded parts of the planet, it has also destroyed some of the natural harbours and fishing waters surrounding Hong Kong.

Even when property rights or environmental issues are not a concern, schemes to expand the supply of housing can be controversial. Existing property owners and local residents are often wary of the impact of any potential development in their own area and, in some countries, have the power to object to proposed changes, thus acting as a further break on change to the housing stock. More generally still, as it is often demographic change that prompts a debate about housing supply, it can often be the case that those unhappy with the changing make-up of society use housing debates as an outlet for their broader objections. In particular, it is not uncommon for the anti-immigration lobby to argue that housing shortages could be reduced if immigration were restricted. Similarly, when some governments have expanded housing provisions, particularly social housing, to cater for the growing number of non-traditional families, socially conservative groups have quite often accused them of facilitating family break-up or encouraging people to act irresponsibly. Sometimes these debates have a particularly pernicious edge, with opponents of change suggesting that migrants, asylum seekers or single parents receive preferential treatment such as access to the best-equipped social housing, much reduced rents or priority in the allocation of vacant properties if there is a waiting list. Almost always these claims are false, but the debates themselves highlight the sensitivity that is often needed when devising housing policies.

Indeed, all of these dilemmas serve to highlight the central point we made at the start of this chapter: that the home is a very personal space. It is because of this that sensitivities can be so fraught. What is more, it also underlines that homes are, of course, centrally embedded within communities and neighbourhoods that often deeply define people's own sense of identity. Housing policy fundamentally shapes the places in which we live and, moreover, has the power to reshape communities too. This power needs to be used respectfully and, often, cautiously. Policy makers need to be aware of the dangers that can arise from poor community planning. In particular, there are dangers that can arise from the segregation of different social groups into different places, be they intended or unintended.

In some of the home-owning dominated systems, the division between owner-occupiers and renters has been a factor contributing to a segregation of different income groups into different neighbourhoods. Often, the response to this duality has been for the government to aim for a further extension of home ownership. This approach is not without its dangers. Most notably, there are questions about the sustainability of a housing market in which mortgage finance is very easily available. High or rising repossession rates can be an indicator that the market has extended too far. In addition, where home ownership has been fuelled by the privatisation of social housing, this can create additional pressures on the market by diminishing the supply of affordable housing. This can both fuel increases in homelessness and be a factor in pushing people towards becoming owner-occupiers at times when they are not really able to afford to do so.

Arguably the most important of all the housing policy dilemmas is that of deciding what the most desirable balance between owning and renting might be. As noted earlier in this chapter, the balance between these elements varies in different types of housing system. It would be wrong to presume that one approach is superior to others or that as national wealth increases that home ownership will naturally be extended. As Figure 6.1 shows, there are dramatic variations in home ownership rates across Europe and, moreover, in the powerhouse economies of Europe we see relatively low levels of ownership in France and Germany, but relatively high levels in Italy and the UK. Interestingly, there seems to be no real pattern in the changing direction of housing tenure in high-income countries since the 1960s either. While some, such as the UK,

Figure 6.1: Home ownership rates in Europe, 2001

% of owner-occupied housing

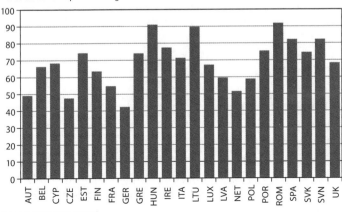

Source: Eurostat (2007)

France and many Eastern European countries, have seen big increases in the level of home ownership, others – such as Japan and Switzerland – have seen home ownership levels drop.

All that said, we should not presume that because there is no 'best' model that choices about the balance between renting and home owning are neutral. As indicated above, the level of home ownership can have wide-ranging consequences for society. Indeed, some theorists have suggested there is a direct link between the level of home ownership within a society and the make-up of its welfare state more generally. Some have even talked of 'the big trade-off' between high levels of home ownership and high levels of welfare spending, pointing to a broad trend in high-income nations towards one or the other (Kemeny, 2005). While this is a contested view, it is suggested that societies with high levels of home ownership may require citizens to invest so much of their income into housing that they are unwilling to tolerate the higher taxes necessary for generous welfare or, on the contrary, that high levels of home ownership are a response to weak welfare states, providing a personal investment-based safety net to protect in times of need.

In short, although housing is seen by some theorists as being at the margins of social policy, particularly in nations where owner occupation dominates, such a view is flawed. Not only is access to housing central to our individual well-being, the very nature of the housing system itself has an impact on how we live our lives, on how we plan for our futures, on our economies and, perhaps, on the very nature of welfare states.

SUMMARY

- ■ **The state has a major role to play** in deciding how much housing needs to be built, what type and size of properties are needed and the control of housing standards.
- ■ Creating a **balance of households to dwellings** is a fundamental aim of housing policy but whether and/or how this is achieved varies according to a country's level of economic development and political traditions.

- Housing differs from the other pillars of welfare because most activity and provision occurs in the **private sector** and a large part of the expenditure on housing is on the physical stock (capital) compared to education or health where continuing to deliver the service is the major cost.

READING GUIDE

Burnett (1986) and Holmans (1987) provide excellent historical accounts of the development of housing policy in the UK, one from the point of view of a social historian, the other written by an economist. Lowe (2004) is the best overview of the subject matter discussed in this chapter with a focus on policy making and taking the same comparative approach adopted here. For students wanting to go to the next level in housing this is the best available source. Bramley et al (2004) is a useful collection of chapters that explore key issues such as the nature of the modern housing market. Mullins and Murie (2006) is the most recent textbook on the UK with a strong bias towards issues in state housing. One of the best insights into the wider comparative focus is Kemeny (1992).

For the UK there are several useful internet sources easily accessed at the government's own housing website, which is part of the Department for Communities and Local Government (www.communities.gov.uk). All the latest statistics, for example on homelessness, and new building housing standards can easily be found, much of it based on the government's continuous Survey of English Housing. The website of the independent research organisation, the Joseph Rowntree Foundation, is the gateway to many sources and contains short versions of the innumerable research studies that they have conducted (www.jrf.org.uk). Similarly, a useful source in its own right but with many links to other sites is the Centre for Housing Policy at the University of York (www.york.ac.uk/inst/chp). These three websites lead to almost all the published information about housing that is available in the UK. At the European level, Eurostat (2007) provides useful information on housing tenure and the European Federation of National Organisations Working with the Homeless (FEANTSA) runs the European Observatory on Homelessness, which provides data on the nature and extent of homelessness in Europe (www.feantsa.org/).

7

conclusion

Introduction

In our short tour of some of the key sights of social policy we have covered much ground: five key pillars of welfare; examples and evidence from more than 70 different countries; some key conceptual arguments; numerous policy issues; and an array of often competing policy mechanisms. Yet we must emphasise that this is only a *short* guide: as we said at the start of the book, we have constrained ourselves to a tour of the major 'boulevards' of social policy. There is, of course, much more to be seen and much more to be said.

So far, we have largely written about the pillars as though they are separate, discreet entities not connected to each other. As we have hinted at at times, this is not in reality the case and as a consequence we have to acknowledge some doubt about discussing them as we have done in separate chapters. Our decision to offer a separate treatment of each pillar simply arises from the fact that this is a short introductory text and we have to begin somewhere. Or, in other words, we need to simplify the often beguiling complexity of the real world in order to offer a less complex analysis of it. However, as we draw the book to a close it is very important that readers realise that:

- there are important interrelationships between the major pillars of welfare discussed;
- the pillars of welfare have a broad significance that extends beyond the issues covered here;

- there are other ways of thinking about welfare spending than our emphasis on pillars and policy mechanisms;
- we have focused our attention on the 'what' questions of social policy (that is, what the pillars look like), but there are important 'why' questions that also need to be addressed (that is, why countries tackle common social problems in different ways).

In this chapter we want to briefly reflect on these points and so will:

- offer some thoughts on how the pillars we have already toured relate to each other;
- highlight the broader dimensions that our key pillars operate within;
- underline the crucial role that broader theoretical perspectives must play in providing an understanding of the 'why' questions in social policy analysis.

The 'five giants' of welfare

Taking our cue from Beveridge (1942), we focused our attention in this short guide on five key pillars of welfare: social security, employment, education, health and housing. Given that we analysed these pillars independently, it is worth us spending a little time reflecting on how they relate to one another. Much social policy research has uncovered significant differences in the nature of welfare states across countries. Despite the fact that they deal with common risks and contingencies, social policies addressing, say, healthcare needs, do not always share the same goals in different countries, with some offering universally available public healthcare and others favouring private provision. Some analysts have suggested that we can see different 'welfare regimes' across the world, with very different types of welfare system in place in different countries around the world (Esping-Andersen, 1990).

Sometimes we take for granted how things work in our own society or our own lives and can fall into the trap of thinking that much of what we see is the norm. The comparison of our own situation with those in other places is a very valuable tool, therefore, for helping us learn about ourselves. This is true for our personal life as well as for the analysis of social policies. For instance, we can only tell whether we are tall or short if we know how we compare to others around us. Equally, we can only know whether a certain country has generous or lean social policies if we compare them to those in other societies. This is the primary reason behind our decision to use a comparative and international approach in this short guide. This is also the reason why – in our mind – the comparative and international social policy research has produced much of the most interesting and thought-provoking work in social policy in recent years.

We should not underestimate the importance of differences between nations' social policies. It is in the detail of social policy mechanisms that we find the fundamental differences of alternative welfare state models and, indeed, fundamental differences in the nature of capitalism within nations. For instance, whether the social security system favours a high degree of income redistribution or simply provides a safety net for a relatively small, targeted group of people tells us a great deal about a nation's (or, perhaps, more accurately, its government's) attitudes towards the allocation of rewards in society and, in turn, its views on the legitimacy of monetary inequalities generated by the free market. We should not forget either that these big macro-level differences in the nature of capitalisms are also played out at the micro-level: differences in social policy mechanisms fundamentally shape people's everyday lives. For example, whether a state takes responsibility for providing comprehensive childcare facilities or whether it allows parents to undertake flexible working hours can influence the chosen career paths of parents and, indeed, influence adults' decisions over whether to have children. For children, different curricula may, for instance, determine the ability to speak different foreign languages, and thus may have an influence on career opportunities in later life. We have discussed many more such examples throughout this book. While we have focused our attention on providing statistical evidence of national differences, it is important to understand that different social policies do not simply alter statistics but have a crucial impact on the everyday-life realities of millions of individuals.

In other words, policy goals and delivery mechanisms are very closely related to each other. A nation that aims to redistribute incomes to a large extent can hardly rely solely on targeted, means-tested benefits. Equally, the aim of status maintenance in conservative countries cannot be achieved by providing very generous universal benefits across the board. While the phrase 'policy mechanisms' may give the impression that social policy is concerned with technical choices between different instruments, we should never lose sight of the fact that these competing mechanisms often embody different values and principles.

We discussed numerous policy issues in our exploration of the pillars. These policy issues also relate – at least to some extent – to the existing delivery mechanisms in different countries. While there is a long-running debate about whether in practice one model of welfare is better than another (see Goodin et al, 1999), it is relatively rare to see nations switch between mechanisms in a radical way. Instead, much policy making in each country involves patching up the weaknesses found within already chosen mechanisms rather than the implementation of alternatives. In other words, because nations have quite different combinations of social policy mechanisms, the nature of policy debate in each country can often be quite different too, even when they are responding to a common crisis or pressure for change such as global economic competition or the ageing of the population. This is an important point, for it suggests that there is rarely one 'right' policy choice that can be pointed to as the best solution for a given problem (Rose, 2005); instead, different countries often require different solutions to similar problems.

Significantly, the policy mechanisms deployed in one pillar of welfare can shape the policy issues faced in another. So, whether a nation actually faces a pensions funding crisis is not only a consequence of the financing mechanism and generosity of pensions but is also – at least partly – caused by increasing life expectancy and persistent low levels of fertility, decisions that may be influenced by health, employment and broader social security policies. The issue of skills shortages is not only caused by processes of deindustrialisation and the growth of the service sector of the labour market but can be facilitated or aggravated by specific focal points in education and migration policies. These examples also help to show that single pillars never work in a vacuum. In reality, every social policy pillar is interacting with each other. So, for example, programmes designed to alleviate poverty in the long run cannot be based solely on income protection schemes: as we have shown, the employment, health, education and housing pillars also have an important role to play. Improvements in the education sector will not alone reach the aim of increasing human development across all segments of society. Equally, the aim of providing an adequate number of dwellings is never simply about housing per se – decisions in this pillar are likely to radiate across all other sectors of policy making as well.

The interconnectedness of many of the key policy dilemmas is one of the reasons why policy delivery is such a complicated aspect of government. It is rarely the case that the state can single-handedly or even in partnership with private market agencies deliver a finished policy solution. One of the major lessons of policy making is that policy can be significantly *remade* during its implementation – by civil servants, by frontline workers, indeed by service users themselves. The policy-making process literature explores issues surrounding the complexity of making policy decisions in the real world in great depth and we should stress here how difficult it is in practice to grapple with very complex and interrelated policy dilemmas (see Hudson and Lowe, 2004). Rarely is there an obvious solution to the key policy issues we have explored here, not least because the interconnectedness of policy pillars in practice makes it difficult to predict how a change in one part of one pillar will impact on the functioning of another part of the same pillar or, indeed, other pillars.

However, what is sometimes overlooked is that *within countries* the respective social security, employment, education, health and housing pillars themselves can function completely differently. While it would make for a very straightforward analysis if some countries had extensive social policies in each pillar of welfare and others minimal social policies in each pillar, the real world shows much more diversity. Indeed, just as governments in different countries make choices about which mechanisms to deploy in each sector, many also make choices over which pillar to bias their investment towards. So, for instance, the US has comparatively high levels of public education spending but low levels of support for unemployed people.

Beyond the five pillars

What all this suggests is that social policies rarely have a very narrow and confined impact nor do they have simple foundations or origins. In fact, it is the very wide-ranging significance and complexity of social policies in the real world that has led to the expanding scope of concern of social policy as an academic subject and, likewise, an increasing interest in social policy among scholars and students of other academic subjects. While, in this guide, we have focused our attention on the traditional 'five giants' of social policy, a fuller exploration of the subject matter would take us into a much broader array of policy areas. Likewise, it would also require us to engage with ideas and debates found in a whole series of related social science subject areas.

As noted in the introductory chapter, the value of a short guide comes in its ability to help the reader locate the major sights and sounds very quickly. However, we recognise that a short guide also carries risks: emphasising the major tourist sights may risk marginalising important landmarks that are off the traditional beaten path; providing context for a short tour might risk simplifying the complex realities of a place; or, worst of all, readers may restrict their tour to the main boulevards described in the guide and decline the invitation to explore further for themselves. In each chapter we have offered guides to further reading when discussing the core pillars. These reading guides will help take you deeper into the detail of the pillars and into topic areas that extend beyond the core themes. Here would we like to broaden our focus a little by briefly highlighting some of the important sights and sounds that lie just outside the main boulevards we have described in the core of this book.

There has long been a strong overlap between the subject matter studied in social work and social policy; indeed, in some countries the two subjects are almost indistinguishable. The core elements of welfare we have explored describe the context within which social workers operate, not least because the lives of the often vulnerable people they support are fundamentally shaped by social policies: how, for example, an individual social worker might address the housing needs of a homeless drug user will, of course, be shaped by the context of the housing policies in place in the specific country or region that the social worker is employed in. Indeed, one of the most challenging questions for social work as a profession is whether part of its task is to campaign for more effective 'supporting' social policies when they feel the existing policies hamper their ability to assist their clients (see Adams, 2002).

While knowledge of social policy is useful for social workers wanting to understand the broader context of their work, the reverse is also true. Indeed, while we restricted this to an exploration of Beveridge's five giants, we could well have added 'social care' or 'social services' as a sixth pillar and analysed the key policy goals, mechanisms and issues of the pillar. For example, how best to provide care for older people is an increasingly prominent debate. The provision of care can take many forms, including residential care for those who might be unable to live in their own home (perhaps due to health reasons for instance) or regular support in a person's own home to help with smaller numbers of tasks that have become more difficult to undertake with age. Such care for older people is usually provided by many different sectors, with state-provided services typically accompanied by a mixture of voluntary services – provided by organisations that raise most of their own funds and provide care to groups of people with specific needs – informal care – unusually provided, unfunded, in the context of families – and private services – run by profit-making companies. This area of policy is also a prime example of where services and pillars overlap; for example, care for older people often interacts with (and depends on) key parts of the social security, housing and health pillars.

On a very similar note, there are also many overlaps between the subjects of criminology and social policy and the two subjects are increasingly studied together (see Knepper, 2007). As with social work, it is evident that knowledge of social policy contexts is vital in aiding understanding of crime and criminal justice. Certainly when we look across nations we can see important variations in, for instance, prison populations, and in the OECD the countries with the highest prison populations tend to be those with the lowest levels of social spending and highest levels of social inequality. While there is no direct link between, say, the levels of crime and inequality in society (and we should always avoid making simple claims that eliminate human choice and agency when discussing social issues), it is clear that social (in)justice is a crucial context within which crime should be understood. Conversely, we should also recognise that social justice is itself influenced by criminal justice not least because a fair and harmonious society offers its citizens not just protection against the risks addressed by Beveridge's five pillars, but also safe and secure communities that are as free from crime as possible.

Less obvious, but increasingly important, links are being made between social policy and geography (see Valentine, 2001) and, similarly, social policy and environmental science (see Huby, 1998). Social policies always have a spatial element in that they are targeted towards a particular country or region. But, more than this, the issues they address often have particularly significant spatial dimensions: unemployment might be higher in particular regions of a country or poverty more heavily concentrated in particular parts of a city for instance. Likewise, debates about sustainable development within environmental science have led to a greater understanding of the interrelationship between social and environmental issues. In particular, there is an increasing recognition that people at higher risk of social exclusion are also often those most likely to live in the most polluted or dangerous areas. Globally it is also largely true that the poorest nations are those most likely to bear the greatest impact of global warming.

Although often seen as polar opposites in the social sciences – one being concerned with markets, the other with the state – there are, in fact, important links to be made between the subjects of economics and social policy and, again, it is not uncommon for the two to be studied together. Certainly, the topics examined by each often heavily overlap: the concern with (un)employment, for example, is central to both, although the manner in which the topic is explored – and the nature of the questions addressed – differ. While, for a long time, a major debate concerned whether extensive social policies might be economically damaging (see Pfaller et al, 1991), there is an increasing recognition that, conversely, social policies themselves might be important economic policies, not least because a well-educated and well-trained workforce is likely to be a more economically competitive one (Giddens, 2000). Political scientists have also had a long-running interest in social policies, not least questions surrounding how social policies are created (see Hudson and Lowe, 2004) and why nations veer towards particular policy solutions (more on which below).

Last, but certainly not least, the subjects of sociology and social policy have always been very closely related. Indeed, in many universities the two subjects are co-located in a single school or department and joint study of the two is commonplace. In part this is because the social issues and social problems that concern sociologists are fundamentally shaped by social policies and, likewise, the social problems and issues that social policies seek to address are connected to the basic structures of our societies and fundamentally shaped by powerful social forces. Throughout our discussion of the pillars we have examined key policy issues that arise from different policy mechanisms. In most cases, these policy issues are connected to the impact of policy on specific social divisions that have long been the concern of sociologists, particularly those surrounding class, disability, gender, 'race' and sexuality. We have only touched the surface of these divisions in this and they certainly merit further investigation by readers, not least because they can offer a powerful alternative lens through which to view policy differences. So, for instance, it has been argued that a gendered perspective on welfare state types might analyse the structure of the 'male-breadwinner' model that underpins much social policy (Lewis, 1992). In many countries welfare provision has been based on the assumption that men go out to work and women stay at home to bring up children. Clearly, such outdated models hold little correlation with the realities of most advanced post-industrial societies in which the workforce is often made up almost equally of women and men, yet social policy mechanisms have often been slow to recognise this and, indeed, in some cases (predominantly male) policy makers have actively reinforced the male breadwinner model. In approaching an analysis of welfare state types from this perspective,

Lewis was able to highlight how different nations used social policies in different ways to influence different roles for men and women. This was a powerful observation, all the more so for the fact that much of the work analysing welfare state types had largely overlooked such differences. In short, social divisions can both influence and be influenced by social policies, so an appreciation of one can clearly aid understanding of the other.

From what to why

Social policy, then, has a wide relevance that stretches far beyond the issues specific to the individual pillars we have discussed. It is precisely because of this that it is such an intellectually stimulating subject and, indeed, why governments face such difficult challenges when trying to devise and implement effective social policy. Social policy matters because it has a real impact on real lives and tackles fundamental political questions about the nature of the good society. The different policy mechanisms that we have examined matter because they embody different goals and values, favour some groups over others and influence the very nature of our societies. In other words, 'what' social policies look like matters. But there also exists a very challenging academic question that goes beyond the 'what' question of 'what do social policies do and look like?' that we have addressed here and, instead, asks the 'why?' question: 'why do different societies adopt different social policy solutions?'. In drawing the book to a close we want to briefly reflect on this 'why?' question by highlighting some of the very significant political science work concerning the 'political economy of welfare' that has looked to address this question.

We have taken our lead in this book from Esping-Andersen (1990; see also, Esping-Andersen, 1999) and we can do so here once again in tackling the 'why?' question. His work was based on the theoretical proposition that the differences between welfare states – and the reason behind the three 'regimes' he identified – were the result of the balance of different political alliances that were made in each country based around the outcome of power struggles between social classes. This is why he called his 'three worlds' 'regimes', a term that has been widely and often wrongly used subsequently. His 'three worlds' are based not on empirical differences that he discovered in his data but on his prior theory of class alliances.

Esping-Andersen argued that there are three basic types of welfare system: a **liberal regime** that offers minimal protection and little redistribution of income beyond providing a basic safety net, meaning the levels of inequality generated by the market largely remain; a **social democratic regime** that offers high levels of protection and redistributes income between social groups with the aim of creating a more equal society; and a **conservative/corporatist regime** that offers high levels of income protection, but only redistributes income between social classes on a modest scale.

More importantly for our purposes here, Esping-Andersen argued that each of these regimes was the outcome of specific historical and cultural conditions, with each nation leaning towards one regime or another on a more-or-less fixed basis. He showed, for example, that societies were more likely to develop a conservative welfare regime if Catholic political parties were comparably strong – that is, if they managed to gain a substantial number of parliamentary and Cabinet seats on a regular basis – and if societies looked back at a comparably strong historical tradition of Absolutism and Authoritarianism. Meanwhile, he suggested that the relatively generous social security solutions in social democratic regime types were typically linked to working-class strength and, moreover, the ability of working-class groups to form lasting political coalitions with middle-class groups. For instance, Esping-Andersen suggested that it was the successful coalitions of Left and Agrarian parties in the Scandinavian countries that helped to broaden the support base – not least within the electorate – for the development of a comprehensive welfare state in those countries. Compared to the social democratic countries, working-class strength remained strictly limited in the liberal regime types. Consequently, the development of generous and universal social security solutions also remained limited. This, of course, is a rather crude summary of Esping-Andersen's thesis, but the key point for our purposes is to stress how important the *historical and cultural foundations* of a society are to the type of welfare system that develops. This argument is closely related to the discovery of the 'three worlds' by Esping-Andersen and more generally to the idea that there are *different solutions to welfare provision* in different nations.

Esping-Andersen's work is part of a more general theoretical stream emanating from political science that emphasises the *power resources* of opposing political groups as an explanation for the wide range of differing social policy frameworks found across nations. Power resource theories have long dominated the comparative and international analysis of social policies. Nevertheless, Esping-Andersen's findings – especially his classification of individual countries to one of the three welfare regime types – have not been uncontested. Esping-Andersen can be criticised for attaching too much importance in his theoretical position to class and class coalitions as a determining factor and also his selective use of data – for example, he did not use housing in his analysis, perhaps because the housing data would not easily fit his threefold model. Not least, one has to keep in mind that his analysis only covers a relatively small number of high-income countries. We have to be careful not to impose his explanations to countries with completely different cultural, historical and economic traditions. Only now are we seeing the first attempts to develop alternative regime types for East Asian, Latin American and African countries around the world (see Gough and Wood, 2004; Walker and Wong, 2005).

Power resource theories also play a major role in the so-called party difference hypotheses. Rather than concentrating on the strength and *couleur* of class coalitions, proponents of party difference explanations point to party political dominance of the legislature and executive across countries (for example, Castles, 1982; Huber and Stephens, 2001). So, for example, scholars would point to the fact that countries in which Left-inclined social democratic parties were successful have had higher spending on welfare state services than those countries with longer-term Right-wing or mixed party political traditions. More refined versions of this very basic assumption have brought forward detailed theories about the very conditions necessary for such an influence to be discernable. The interdependence of Left- and Right-wing parties in their competition for electoral votes has been mentioned here. Equally, scholars have pointed to the important role different political systems can play in shaping party influence (for example, Immergut, 1992; Pierson, 1995). Thus, it is argued, it matters whether parties compete in a parliamentary or a presidential system; it matters whether they compete in a federalist or a centralist system; whether there are many or only a few parties – all these structural differences have an influence on the policy-making process, may favour certain interests over others and therefore have an influence on the scope and functioning of the social pillars. These institutional approaches have gained much attention in contemporary debates about the reform of welfare states (Pierson, 2001).

Closely related to institutional explanations of the development and change of the welfare pillars are explanations that emphasise policy inheritance or **path dependency** (Hudson and Lowe, 2004; Pierson, 2004). For instance, as we have shown, the liberal, conservative and social democratic welfare regime types produce very dissimilar policy mechanisms; these dissimilarities are said to in turn produce repercussions for the policy-making process. So, for example, at the very start of the book we began by describing the intense debate over healthcare reform in the US. Despite the fact that the healthcare system there is deemed inadequate by many – not least because it fails to provide coverage to millions of its citizens, including a large proportion of North American children – the system has proved highly resistant to reform. In large part this is because those who benefit most from the status quo – including the powerful private health insurance funds and private healthcare providers – are unlikely to endorse reforms that radically extend the role of the state and so threaten their role, their power and their profits. Yet, in many other countries, it is taken as a given that the state *should* be the main provider of healthcare, not least because the state has undertaken such a role for many decades. The broader theoretical argument here is that policy mechanisms can *shape* political interests as well as reflecting them, so early policy choices can be hard to change as a consequence. This is the main idea behind the notion that each nation's policies are often 'path dependent': once they go down a particular direction of development they can prove hard to reverse later.

Theoretical arguments of this sort are often omitted from introductory guides to social policy, but we introduce them here because we believe the 'why?' questions matter as much as the 'what?' questions. Indeed, without a conceptual foundation mere comparison of data is not particularly meaningful; indeed it is not possible to make true comparisons without some sort of theory. The emphasis in the previous chapters on the vast differences in the way the five pillars are organised and underpinned by different ideas of individuality, social solidarity and the role of the state across countries is very interesting in its own right. However, while we may be able to show how a number of countries differ in, say, their approach to child poverty or spending on health services, we are unable to say why they differ without some recourse to theory. While addressing the 'what?' questions – providing a guide map through the possibilities and limitations of social policy across the globe – is a sensible starting point for our tour of social policy, students interested in understanding the 'sense' behind the statistics and structural characteristics of comparative and international social policies have to take their short guide through social policy a stage further by also considering the 'why?' questions.

Conclusion

All people across the world share more or less the same fundamental human needs; indeed, the belief that this is so underpins the *Universal Declaration of Human Rights* (UN Assembly, 1948; www.un.org/rights/) that we have cited on various occasions throughout our discussion of the pillars of welfare. Modern social policies can play a hugely significant role in the delivery of human rights, but a key lesson highlighted in this book is that *how* this is achieved varies very considerably from country to country. Comparative welfare state research has shown that there are three or four basic models of provision but that each country has its own unique features. Moreover, we should not presume that social policies always meet essential human needs as fully as they might do or that the social rights of all people in a society are met equally: welfare states vary in their expansiveness and in the degree to which they aim to address social divisions and social inequalities.

In this book we have emphasised the value of looking beyond a single country when thinking about social policy issues. The broader perspective that can be found by considering examples from different countries helps to sharpen our thinking about the nature of each pillar, the possibilities of social policy and the challenges policy makers face. If you are German, American, Chinese, Brazilian – wherever you come from in fact – it can be natural to presume that the country you have experienced is the 'norm'. Looking at a range of different countries can usefully challenge presumptions about what is normal and what is possible. However, we have also emphasised here the importance of social theory in helping us to understand social policy. Facts and figures cannot tell us everything on their own and an example taken out of context can be misleading too. We should not, therefore, be too single-minded in our analysis of social policies. In particular, we should reflect on why nations differ and how far policy differences are a consequence of long-run cultural, economic, political and institutional differences of nations. What this means in practice is that we should not presume that policies can easily be moved between nations: while, for instance, you might decide that Sweden, Denmark or Germany has a better social security policy framework than your own country, you should not necessarily conclude that your country should immediately adopt the approach found in one of those countries. Instead, you might want to ask first why the policy differences exist and to think about the broader factors that might lead your country to having what you regard as a less desirable policy framework.

Of course, in order to undertake such a reflection you will most likely find it useful to extend your short tour of social policy into a much longer one. We should emphasise here once again the point that this short book is only a first step for readers new to this fascinating subject and we make no claim to have written a full, once-and-for-all account of social policy. At the start of the book we said that our aim was to guide you through the main 'boulevards' of social policy and to point out the most famous 'tourist' sites. Just as any good guidebook ought to, we hope that our brief tour has whetted your appetite for a further trip to cover the other parts of the territory. The first time you visit a city it is useful to know what the main buildings are called and where they are located, but much more can be gained on subsequent visits by scratching beneath this surface and learning more about the history of the buildings, the political debates that surrounded their construction or the social and environmental impact of their construction. In exploring the five main pillars we have given you a short overview of social policy. However, we concluded each chapter with an indication of some of the core reading that can take you further in your travels and, below, we do so again for the broader themes raised in this concluding chapter. We have now given you that first tour round the 'city' of social policy; we hope that we have inspired you to explore it further.

READING GUIDE

An accessible starting point for those wanting to explore the 'why?' question is Hudson and Lowe's (2004) *Understanding the policy process*; this text was written by two authors of this guide and very much starts off where the guide finishes so is a natural companion to this book. Esping-Andersen's (1990) classic *The three worlds of welfare capitalism* is essential reading for those wanting to know more about welfare state types. It has been much critiqued in recent years – see Arts and Gelissen (2002) for an overview of the debate. Gough and Wood (2004) and Walker and Wong (2005) provide useful discussions of welfare regimes in some of the regions neglected in Esping-Andersen's original work.

references

Adams, R. (2002) *Social policy for social work*, Basingstoke: Palgrave.

Adema, W. and Ladaique, M. (2005) *Net social expenditure, 2005 edition: More comprehensive measures of social support*, OECD Social, Employment and Migration Working Papers, Paris: OECD.

Arts, W. A. and Gelissen, J. (2002) 'Three worlds of welfare capitalism or more? A state-of-the-art report', *Journal of European Social Policy*, vol 12, no 2, pp 137-48.

Asian Development Bank (2007) *Key indicators 2007: Inequality in Asia*, accessible at: www.adb.org/Documents/Books/Key_Indicators/2007/default.asp

Bachelard, G. (1992) *The poetics of space*, Boston, MA: Beacon Press.

Baggott, R. (2007) *Understanding health policy*, Bristol: The Policy Press.

Bambra, C. (2005) 'Worlds of welfare and the health care discrepancy', *Social Policy & Society*, vol 4, no 1, pp 31-41.

Beveridge, W.H.B. (1942) *Social insurance and allied services*, Basingstoke: Macmillan.

Blanden, J., Gregg, P. and Machin, S. (2005) *Intergenerational mobility in Europe and North America: A report supported by the Sutton Trust*, London: LSE Centre for Economic Performance.

Blank, R.H. and Burau, V.D. (2007) *Comparative health policy*, Basingstoke: Palgrave Macmillan.

Bramley, G., Munro, M. and Pawson, H. (2004) *Key issues in housing: Policies and markets in 21st-century Britain*, Basingstoke: Palgrave Macmillan.

Burnett, J. (1986) *A social history of housing, 1815-1985*, London: Routledge.

Burrows, R., Pleace, N. and Quilgars, D. (1997) *Homelessness and social policy*, London: Routledge.

Carpenter, M., Freda, B. and Speeden, S. (eds) (2007) *Beyond the workfare state: Labour markets, equalities and human rights*, Bristol, The Policy Press.

Castles, F.G. (1982) *The impact of parties: Politics and policies in democratic capitalist states*, London: Sage Publications.

Castles, F.G. (2007) *The disappearing state?: Retrenchment realities in an age of globalization*, Cheltenham: Edward Elgar.

Chan, C. K. and Bowpitt, G. (2005) *Human dignity and welfare systems*, Bristol: The Policy Press.

Clasen, J. (1997) *Social insurance in Europe*, Bristol: The Policy Press.

Committee of Inquiry into a Comprehensive System of Social Security (2002) *Inquiry into the various social security aspects of the South African health system*, Pretoria: South African Department of Health.

Crouch, C., Finegold, D. and Sako, M. (1999) *Are skills the answer?: The political economy of skill creation in advanced industrial countries*, Oxford: Oxford University Press.

Ditch, J. (1999) *Introduction to social security: Policies, benefits, and poverty*, London: Routledge.

Dwyer, P. (2004) *Understanding social citizenship: Themes and perspectives for policy and practice*, Bristol: The Policy Press.

Edgar, B. and Meert, H. (2006) *Fifth review of statistics on homelessness*, Brussels: FEANTSA.

Esping-Andersen, G. (1990) *The three worlds of welfare capitalism*, Cambridge: Polity Press.

Esping-Andersen, G. (1999) *Social foundations of postindustrial economies*, Oxford: Oxford University Press.

European Commission (2002) *Continuing training in enterprises in Europe: Results of the second European Continuing Vocational Training Survey in enterprises*, Brussels: European Commission.

European Industrial Relations Observatory (2007) *EIROnline*, accessible at: www.eurofound.europa.eu/

Eurostat (2007) *Statistics portal of the statistical office of the European Communities*, accessible at: http://epp.eurostat.ec.europa.eu/

Froggett, L. (2002) *Love, hate and welfare: Psychosocial approaches to policy and practice*, Bristol: The Policy Press.

Fu, T. (2006) 'Taiwan', *Policy World*, issue 6.

Giddens, A. (1991) *Modernity and self-identity: Self and society in the late modern age,* Cambridge: Polity Press.

Giddens, A. (2000) *The third way and its critics*, Cambridge: Polity Press.

Glennerster, H. (2003) *Understanding the finance of welfare: What welfare costs and how to pay for it*, Bristol: The Policy Press.

Goodin, R.E., Headey, B., Muffels, R. and Dirven, H. (1999) *The real worlds of welfare capitalism*, Cambridge: Cambridge University Press.

Gough, I. and Wood, G.D. (2004) *Insecurity and welfare regimes in Asia, Africa and Latin America: Social policy in development contexts*, Cambridge: Cambridge University Press.

Goul Andersen, J. and Jensen, P.H. (2002) *Changing labour markets, welfare policies and citizenship*, Bristol: The Policy Press.

Ham, C. (2004) *Health policy in Britain: The politics and organisation of the National Health Service*, Basingstoke: Palgrave Macmillan.

Hayward, G. and James, S. (2004) *Balancing the skills equation: Key issues and challenges for policy and practice*, Bristol: The Policy Press.

Henman, P. and Fenger, M. (eds) (2006) *Administering welfare reform: International transformations in welfare governance,* Bristol: The Policy Press.

Holmans, A.E. (1987) *Housing policy in Britain: A history*, London: Croom Helm.

Holmans, A.E. (2000) 'British housing in the twentieth century: an end-of-century overview', in S. Wilcox (ed) *Housing finance review 1999-2000*, York/Coventry: Joseph Rowntree Foundation/Chartered Institute of Housing and the Council of Mortgage Lenders.

Huber, E. and Stephens, J.D. (2001) *Development and crisis of the welfare state: Parties and policies in global markets*, Chicago, IL: University of Chicago Press.

Huby, M. (1998) *Social policy and the environment*, Buckingham: Open University Press.

Hudson, J. and Lowe, S. (2004) *Understanding the policy process: Analysing welfare policy and practice*, Bristol: The Policy Press.

ILO (International Labour Organization) (2007) *ILO labour force statistics*. Geneva: ILO.

IMF (International Monetary Fund) (2007a) *World Economic Outlook database*, accessible at: www.imf.org/external/ns/cs.aspx?id=28

IMF (2007b) *IMF Government Finance Statistics*, accessible at: www.esds.ac.uk/international/support/user_guides/imf/gfs.asp

Immergut, E.M. (1992) *Health politics: Interests and institutions in Western Europe*, Cambridge: Cambridge University Press.

Johnson, N. (1987) *The welfare state in transition: The theory and practice of welfare pluralism*, London: Harvester Wheatsheaf.

Kemeny, J. (1981) *The myth of home-ownership: Private versus public choices in housing tenure*, London: Routledge & Kegan Paul.

Kemeny, J. (1992) *Housing and social theory*, London: Routledge.

Kemeny, J. (2005) '"The really big trade-off" between home ownership and welfare: Castles' evaluation of the 1980 thesis, and a reformulation 25 years on', *Housing and Social Theory*, vol 22, no 2, pp 59-85.

Knepper, P. (2007) *Criminology and social policy*, London: Sage Publications.

Lewis, J. (1992) 'Gender and the development of welfare regimes', *Journal of European Social Policy*, vol 2, no 3, pp 159-73.

Lødemel, I. and Trickey, H. (2001) *'An offer you can't refuse': Workfare in international perspective*, Bristol: The Policy Press.

Lowe, S. (2004) *Housing policy analysis: British housing in cultural and comparative context*, Basingstoke: Palgrave Macmillan.

Lowe, S. and Tsenkova, S. (2003) *Housing change in East and Central Europe: Integration or fragmentation*, Aldershot: Ashgate.

McKeown, T. (1979) *The role of medicine: Dream, mirage or nemesis?*, Oxford: Blackwell.

Marshall, T. H. (1950) *Citizenship and social class, and other essays*, Cambridge: Cambridge University Press.

Millar, J. (ed) (2003) *Understanding social security: Issues for policy and practice*, Bristol: The Policy Press.

MISSOC (Mutual Information System on Social Protection) (2007) *Mutual Information System on Social Protection in the member states of the EU*, accessible at: http://ec.europa.eu/employment_social/social_protection/index_en.htm

Mooney, G. (ed) (2004) *Work: Personal lives and social policy*, Bristol: The Policy Press.

Mullins, D. and Murie, A. (2006). *Housing policy in the UK*, Basingstoke: Palgrave Macmillan.

Nettleton, S. (2006) *The sociology of health and illness*, Cambridge: Polity Press.

OECD (Organisation for Economic Co-operation and Development) (2003) *OECD PISA (Programme for International Student Assessment) 2003*, accessible at: www.pisa.oecd.org/

OECD (2004) *Proposal for a taxonomy of health insurance: OECD study on private health insurance*, Paris: OECD.

OECD (2005a) *Pensions at a glance*, Paris: OECD.

OECD (2005b) *Society at a glance*, Paris: OECD.

OECD (2006a) *Benefits and wages: Gross/net replacement rates, country specific files and tax/benefit models*, Paris: OECD.

OECD (2006b) *Society at a glance*, Paris: OECD.

OECD (2007a) *Social Expenditure Database (SOCX)*, Paris: OECD.

OECD (2007b) *Education at a glance*, Paris: OECD.

OECD (2007c) *OECD health data*, Paris: OECD.

Olssen, M., Codd, J. and O'Neill, A.-M. (2004) *Education policy: Globalization, citizenship and democracy*, London: Sage Publications.

Pfaller, A., Gough, I. and Therborn, G. (1991) *Can the welfare state compete? A comparative study of five advanced capitalist countries*, Basingstoke: Macmillan.

Pierson, P. (1995) 'Fragmented welfare states: federalism and the development of social policy', *Governance*, vol 8, pp 449-78.

Pierson, P. (2001) *The new politics of the welfare state*, Oxford: Oxford University Press.

Pierson, P. (2004) *Politics in time: History, institutions, and social analysis*, Princeton, NJ: Princeton University Press.

Powell, M.A. (ed) (2007) *Understanding the mixed economy of welfare*, Bristol: The Policy Press.

Ridge, T. and Wright, S. (eds) (2008) *Understanding inequality, poverty and wealth: Policies and prospects*, Bristol: The Policy Press.

Rose, R. (2005) *Learning from comparative public policy: A practical guide*, London: Routledge.

Saraceno, C. (2002) *Social assistance dynamics in Europe: National and local poverty regimes*, Bristol: The Policy Press.

Scruggs, L. (2005) *Comparative welfare entitlements dataset*, accessible at: www.sp.uconn.edu/~scruggs/wp.htm

Smith, G.D. (2003) *Health inequalities: Lifecourse approaches*, Bristol: The Policy Press.

SSA (Social Security Administration) (2007) *Social security programs throughout the world*, accessible at: www.ssa.gov/policy/docs/progdesc/ssptw/

Tawney, R.H. (1931) *Equality*, London: Allen & Unwin.

Titmuss, R.M. (1956) *The social division of welfare*, Liverpool: Liverpool University Press.

Titmuss, R.M. (1958) *Essays on 'the welfare state'*, London: Allen & Unwin.

Tomlinson, S. (2005) *Education in a post-welfare society*, Maidenhead: Open University Press.

UNDP (United Nations Development Programme) (2007) *Human development report 2007/8: Fighting climate change: Human solidarity in a divided world*, New York: Palgrave Macmillan, accessible at: www.undp.org/

UNESCO/OECD (United Nations Educational, Scientific and Cultural Organization/Organisation for Economic Co-operation and Development) (2007) *World education indicators*, accessible at: http://stats.uis.unesco.org/

UN (United Nations) General Assembly (1948) *Universal Declaration of Human Rights*, Lake Success, NY: UN Department of Public Information.

Valentine, G. (2001) *Social geographies: Society and space*, Harlow: Longman.

van Berkel, R. and Møller, I. H. (2002) *Active social policies in the EU: Inclusion through participation?*, Bristol: The Policy Press.

Walker, A. and Wong, C.-K. (2005) *East Asian welfare regimes in transition: From Confucianism to globalisation*, Bristol: The Policy Press.

Walker, R. and Howard, M. (2000) *The making of a welfare class?: Benefit receipt in Britain*, Bristol: The Policy Press.

WHO (World Health Organisation) (2007) *World Health Organisation Statistical Information System*, accessible at: www.who.int/whosis/en/index.html

World Bank (2007) *World development indicators*, accessible at: http://web.worldbank.org/WBSITE/EXTERNAL/DATASTATISTICS/
0,,contentMDK:20535285~menuPK:1192694~pagePK:64133150~piPK:64133175~theSitePK:239419,00.html

index